# Finding the Facts

## What Every Workplace
## Investigator Needs to Know

# Finding the Facts

## What Every Workplace Investigator Needs to Know

Fran A. Sepler

**Ventana, LLC**
Saint Louis Park, Minnesota

First printing 2008

ISBN 978-0-9817397-2-4

LCCN 2008929739

# Table of Contents

# Foreword

*Finding the Facts: What Every Workplace Investigator Needs to Know* is truly an A-to-Z guide to workplace investigations. In it, Fran Sepler draws on years of practical experience as an investigator, supplemented by her own research and insights into employee psychology and organizational dynamics. This book is well-organized, clearly written, and highly practical. Its frequent scenarios used to illustrate points have the ring of authenticity, and keep the reader involved. Ms. Sepler seemingly covers every imaginable issue related to investigation, providing detailed suggestions and lists, right down to details such as how to prepare the interview room and where to have the subject sit.

I recommend *Finding the Facts* to readers with a wide variety of connections to the workplace investigation process. Its breadth and depth is such that even highly experienced investigators will discover new ideas and perspectives, while those with less experience will find it a confidence-building introduction to the process that immediately becomes a reference to turn to repeatedly during investigations. At the policymaking and planning level, this book offers a basis from which to prepare a companywide approach to investigations that ensures consistency, fairness, thoroughness, and reduces legal risk.

As a labor and employment attorney, I typically see workplace investigations from a bit of a distance—and all too often only after the fact. From that perspective, I definitely recommend *Finding the Facts* to my professional peers, both for its utility in guiding clients through investigations and for its independent value in litigation. Although there are certainly major differences between conducting an investigation and developing a case for trial, significant portions of this book could be quite useful to employment lawyers performing vital tasks such as conducting depositions, defending or attacking the completeness and fairness of particular investigations at issue in litigation, and assessing and arguing all-important credibility issues.

*George Lenard, managing partner,*
*Harris Dowell Fisher & Harris*
*author, George's Employment Blawg*

# Acknowledgments

Discretion is a workplace fact-finder's stock in trade. I therefore thank collectively the many attorneys, human resources professionals, and organizational leaders who have entrusted me with their challenging cases.

Special thanks to George Lenard for his generous words, to Sue Collier for her talents and wisdom, Joseph Nierenberg for his patient feedback and support, and to Jeff Johnson and Colleen Sheffler for many years of opportunity to teach what I love.

# Introduction

The impetus for an investigation is almost always a report or a complaint. Someone has informed the organization that something is not the way it should be. The organization now "knows" of the possibility that something is "amiss" and must make a decision about its own behavior. Since the actions the organization may take— or refrain from taking—create at least as much exposure for the organization as the situation, incident, behavior, or relationship being complained about, the organization has a stake in finding out the precise nature of the situation, incident, behavior, or relationship. This is the first premise of competent investigations. *An investigation is not an effort to prove or disprove allegations, or to determine whether allegations are true, but to use them as a starting point to determine "what happened" or "what is happening."* Although this may appear to be a subtle distinction, it should guide every step of an investigation. An employment investigator has a duty to look beyond simple incidents or utterances to examine the situation as a whole, while at the same time not scrutinizing so wide a swath of organizational life as to fulfill the inevitable charge that one is "on a witch hunt."

Discipline, expertise, and steadfast attention to purpose are required if one is to be the eyes and ears of the organization, to gather intelligence and facts that are helpful, and to neutralize the negative impact of an investigation by balancing it with information that promotes fairness and consistency. It also calls for knowledge of human psychology, organizational theory, law, and business administration. Since it is the rare investigator who has formally studied each of these, this guide will bring the essential elements of investigative wisdom together, to prepare and guide you through the complexities and possibilities of employment investigations.

This book is organized to help any investigator improve any part of his or her practice, and to clarify and pull apart the structural and strategic elements of an effective investigation. The final chapter provides a psychological primer for investigators interested in understanding some of the underlying dynamics particular to harassment and discrimination complaints, and the implications of these dynamics for investigators in these complex cases. In some ways, the final chapter is the "prereading" for understanding the methodology recommended for successful investigations.

Figure 1 lays out the various components of an employment investigation and the actions necessary at each stage of the process. The chapters that follow will provide guidance on meeting the requirements and challenges of each stage, as well as perspective on larger challenges, such as confidentiality and the psychology of the parties being interviewed.

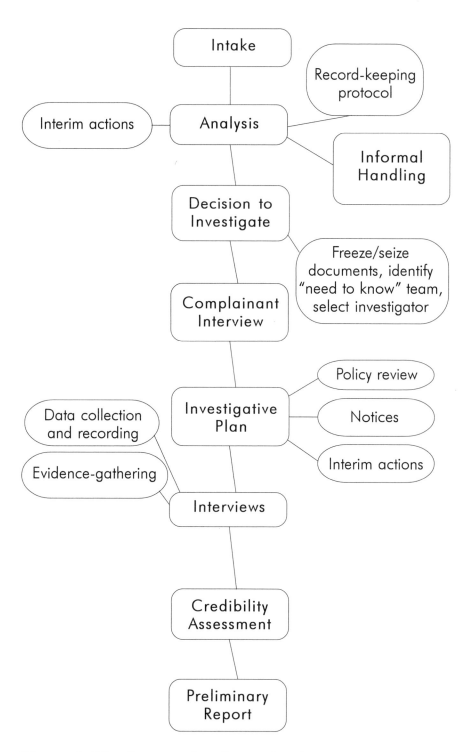

**Figure 1: The Stages of an Investigation**

# CHAPTER 1

# The Many Purposes of an Investigation

If you ask most professionals involved with an employment investigation about its purpose, the answer you are likely to hear is "to find facts." Investigations are indeed intended to determine particulars, but they also serve other purposes that should guide decision-making as an investigation is contemplated.

**Fairness:** A well-done investigation provides visible evidence that an organization not only takes employee concerns seriously, but that it diligently researches the allegation to determine what has actually transpired in the past or what the current situation actually is. This builds confidence in those who are aware of the investigation, reassuring them that if they are concerned about an issue, it will be taken seriously. It also works against the often popular notion that employers summarily fire people based on unsubstantiated allegations.

This aspect of investigations cannot be underestimated, and investigators should be mindful of their mega-impact as they conduct interviews and seek evidence. Maintaining an open mind rather than adopting a prosecutorial demeanor is a high priority, both for purposes of building confidence in the organization's fairness as well as ensuring a clear and defensible investigative outcome.

**Document/memorialize:** Neither human beings nor organizations have infinite memory. Although a particular investigation might consume the organization and the investigator for a period of time, or might seem during the course of the investigation to be unforgettable, the simple reality is that in months or years, the details and even the main theme of an investigation can be difficult to retrieve. In today's world, the point at which it will be most important to carefully recount an organization's response to a complaint—during discovery in litigation or in an administrative hearing—is fairly far out in time from the investigation itself. The parties who did the investigation may by then have moved from the organization, or if they are still present, may have conducted tens or hundreds of investigations since the one in question. Investigating, using a particular protocol, and maintaining a consistent process allows for a routine and detailed manner of ensuring that "organizational memory" is thorough and accurate.

**Proactivity:** There are times when an investigation is, in the context of organizational development, an intervention in its own right. Sometimes an investigator is not investigating a specific allegation but a question of "why?" Why are individuals of a protected class leaving this division in high numbers? Why are there repeated complaints of inappropriate conduct even though prior allegations have not been substantiated? Why are engagement scores so terribly low among women? Some colleagues might argue that an investigation into these types of questions is more properly designated an "assessment," and might be conducted according to somewhat different rules. It is best to proceed with caution, however, as claims of "hostile environment" based on protected class or allegations of systemic discrimination require the same standards as investigations into specific allegations. The difference is that these investigations will involve a greater number of individuals and will sometimes come after many have engaged the problem-solving mechanisms of the organization seeking assistance or expressing concern. Thus, unlike the more "secret" investigation into a specific incident, this type of scrutiny can be a positive sign of the intention of "getting to the bottom" of a problem.

**Meet requirements:** It goes without saying that under certain circumstances, organizations are *required* to conduct investigations. These requirements may stem from the organization's own policies or from state or federal law.

**Shared understanding:** Leaders and decision-makers in organizations are human. They have their own perspectives, prejudices, preferences, and assumptions, which shape their perspective on what is happening within an organization. Often, teams of leaders are like the blind men describing the elephant, with each seeing the nature of situations or even the organization itself from their own unique perspective. When these leaders are faced with organizational challenges, an investigation provides a single analysis and conclusions about an incident or situation. It becomes a source of unified understanding for purposes of decision-making.

A large medical clinic received a complaint of misconduct by one of its highly popular physicians. The complaint polarized the board of directors, with many jumping in to attack the accused and others rising to defend him. Clear that they were not in a position to "figure things out" themselves, they jointly selected an outside investigator. They resolved that they would all use the results of the investigation as the only basis for decision-making. Because of the intense feelings and opinions of all board members, the investigator interviewed each board member to ensure that all relevant information was considered (and to some degree to guarantee a perception of fairness). When the findings were somewhere between what each camp expected, the organization was able to move forward in a rational, balanced way, with all board members agreeing to support the findings of the investigation.

**To ensure that facts are understood in context:** We have all had the experience of being told a truth, only to find out sufficient detail had been omitted.

> To emphasize the poor character of a colleague, a witness reports that the colleague has admitted to being in possession of illegal drugs. A careful investigation finds that in the discussion in question, the individual had spoken about confiscating marijuana from his teenage son and turning it in to the police department.

Facts alone do not always tell the story necessary to understand the behavior or situation. It is insufficient to state that Mary asked Joe to dinner without describing the situation fully. Were Joe and Mary working late? Was it a business dinner? Was anyone else invited? Was the invitation to a romantic restaurant? Investigations rescue organizations from simple-mindedness by ensuring not only that facts are found, but also that they are placed in the proper context so they can be properly analyzed and good decisions can be made.

# CHAPTER 2

# The Competent Organization – Organizational Preparedness

## Organizational preparedness

Some large organizations routinely conduct investigations and have well-established policies and procedures, careful protocol, and guidelines for investigators to follow. Many, however, do not. Even huge companies sometimes allow each investigator to pursue matters using his or her own individual expertise and preferences. Although this may never cause a problem, it does create a significant vulnerability should the organization's practices be carefully scrutinized and the inconsistency identified as a form of sloppiness—or even worse, bias.

Since the majority of organizations do not have full-time investigators, and many conduct only a few investigations each year, it is not necessary for every organization to have elaborate manuals and procedures regarding investigation. Nevertheless, there are certain steps organizations should take to prepare themselves to conduct high-quality investigations and to ensure a reasonable level of consistency from investigation to investigation.

**Policy requiring cooperation:** One of the most frustrating things that can happen in an investigation is the refusal of a key individual to cooperate. Especially when the investigator has reason to believe that the individual can provide essential data, it is important to have leverage to convince him or her to be forthcoming. Although there are a variety of strategies investigators can use to be persuasive, employers should have policies in place that require employees to cooperate with employer-initiated investigations. Even though policies are only words on paper, and threats of discipline for failing to cooperate should only be used as a last resort, this type of policy sets an expectation and a tone that is helpful in orienting employees to their duty to their employer. Employers with unionized employees should take note that some unions have asserted that the requirement for cooperation necessitates that union representation be proffered for all investigative interviews involving bargaining unit members, since refusal to answer a single question could, in their estimation, constitute non-cooperation and result in discipline. Organizations have variously responded by narrowing their definition of "cooperation," by allowing broader representation, or by disagreeing with this assessment and entertaining grievances on this.

**Identify an organizational clearinghouse:** Complaints are made throughout organizations, and each one calls for analysis and decision-making about what steps should be taken to address the situation. Although most organizations are leery of micromanagement, the risks associated with a poorly conducted investigation call for a process in which decisions are *at least* reviewed, if not made in collaboration with a key person with a high-level view of the organization's past action. By reviewing current plans and methods, that person can ensure both consistency and appropriateness of response. Called an "investigative coordinator" in some organizations, this person (or persons) receives reports from all intakes and reviews any action taken. This person then decides whether to catalogue the matter as being appropriately handled at the level closest to the employee, to contact the party who conducted the intake for further information and consultation, or to recommend the matter be formally investigated immediately. This individual is also responsible for determining whether an internal or external investigator would be appropriate.

**Positions and declarations:** There are a number of investigative practices that are controversial; there are legitimate differences of opinion as to whether certain steps should be taken and certain methods used. Organizations should have firm positions on these matters, and they should be observed in each and every investigation that is conducted. Exceptions should be rare and well documented.

1. *Tape recording:* Although under certain collective bargaining agreements or public laws, recording is required in employment investigations, it is optional in most work environments. Experts disagree on the value and importance of making electronic recordings of investigative interviews. Those who favor them like the absolute certainty that there can be independent verification of what was said and the convenience of reviewing the tapes rather than relying on note-taking. Opponents argue that recordings can provide fodder for manipulation ("What was happening during that long pause?"). Whether or not an organization records interviews, there should be consistency in this practice. If tape recordings are to be made, there should be clear technical requirements and ample equipment available. Protocol for storage of tape recordings must be established (i.e., encryption standards for digital recordings). Most importantly, if recordings are to be made, they must be made for every interview conducted within an investigation.

2. *File review:* Investigators find that reviewing personnel files can be illuminating and helpful for a variety of reasons; the timing of the review can also be important. If an investigator routinely examines personnel files prior to interviewing parties, information might come to his or her attention that could be highly prejudicial and create bias.

Gerry has made a claim of inappropriate conduct toward his supervisor. In a routine review of his file, you find that he was suspended two years ago for coming to work under the influence of alcohol.

Although one can declare that he or she is able to put aside impressions gained from possibly unrelated information, it can be argued that avoiding the situation altogether is preferable. Therefore, some organizations instruct investigators to review personnel files only after interviewing the subject. The argument against this, however, is that should the file reveal substantive and previously undisclosed information, a second interview might be necessary, thereby making the procedure less efficient. As with tape recording, this is an endlessly debatable matter, but organizations should have firm procedures for the timing of personnel file scrutiny.

3. *Prior investigations*: There are times when an investigator may be asked to look into a matter that has already been investigated, or a matter that stems from a new allegation that is similar to one that has already been investigated. This means that there should be a complete investigative file in the possession of the organization. Although it is tempting to review data that have already been collected, this should be avoided in order to ensure that the investigation being commenced is neutral, uninfluenced by prior fact-finding. The only document that might be appropriate to examine would be prior written complaints or communication from the complainant or respondent; looking at notes or reports should be avoided until a need to review those documents has been identified.

4. *Number of investigators*: Organizations may wish to institute a policy that all interviews are conducted with two investigators present, particularly if investigators are not highly experienced. Usually

this is structured so one individual asks the questions while the other serves as a mute observer and note-taker. Some organizations believe that putting two investigators in a room with one subject can be intimidating and put a damper on the rapport and intimacy necessary for an investigative interview. Defining the circumstances under which "two-on-one" and "one-on-one" interviews are conducted is essential, as well as guidelines that ensure that within a particular investigation, the composition of the investigative unit (a single person or a team) is consistent from beginning to end.

5.  *Document retention and destruction:* Much can be made about the contents of an investigative file, and organizations should ensure that from one matter to another an investigative file should contain similar documents. Most important, there should be clear standards for retaining and destroying documents. Many investigators "clean up" or "fill in" their notes immediately following an interview. For instance, someone who has used abbreviations might fill in the full words to ensure they will properly recall what was said—or misspellings might be corrected in notes made on a computer. It is essential that investigators have clear guidelines regarding the retention of prior versions of notes under these circumstances, and it is generally recommended that those prior versions be retained. Other record retention issues include the proper designation and labeling of documents considered to be privileged, the retention of drafts of reports or memoranda, and the appropriate handling of documents and items examined but which must be returned or otherwise disposed of.

6.  *Third-party presence:* The presence of a third party (or a fourth party in the case of two-on-one interviews) is sometimes outside an organization's

control, such as an employee exercising Weingarten[1] rights in a union setting. Many organizations, however, relinquish what control they do have unnecessarily or by default. A careful review of Weingarten leaves several issues in the hands of the employer; for instance, an employer is not under any obligation to inform an individual of the right to the presence of a union representative unless that has been agreed to contractually. An employer has reasonable control of the interaction between the union representative and the employee during the interview. Some organizations take the position that you can never give employees too many rights, and provide notice to employees prior to or at the time of the interview that they are entitled to union representation.

Others live by the letter of the law and provide representation only when it is requested in accordance with Weingarten. This is a matter of organizational policy and philosophy. Inconsistency in this area is problematic and should be avoided by taking a clear and organized approach to union representation. This should include seating arrangements (Will the union representative sit next to or behind the employee?) and protocol for allowing consultation or participation (Under what circumstances can the union representative initiate a consultation?). In nonunion environments, employers have broad discretion regarding whether and when employees might have a "support person" or "witness." Some argue that this permission creates

---

[1] *NLRB v. J Weingarten, Inc.* 420 U.S. 251 (1975) provides that "an exclusive representative of an appropriate unit in an agency shall be given the opportunity to be represented at any examination of an employee in the unit by a representative of the agency in connection with an investigation if—(i) the employee reasonably believes that the examination may result in disciplinary action against the employee; and (ii) the employee requests representation."

a higher level of faith in the investigation for employees, and they point out that employees rarely exercise the permission if it is given. Others believe that an uninvolved third party's presence merely increases the risk of information being shared inappropriately and that it does not offer any benefit to the organization or the parties. Finally, most organizations take the position that attorneys are not permitted to be present when the employees they represent are interviewed in an internal investigation; however, when the employee's cooperation hinges on the presence of the attorney, some exceptions are made. It is important to have the individual or individuals who can authorize such exceptions clearly indicated. In many organizations, the decision is made that if an attorney must be present for an essential interview to occur, in-house counsel will also be present.

**Consistent forms and notices:** Organizations are well served by creating forms to ensure investigative consistency and integrity. Although it is not necessary to fill out a form for every step of an investigation, organizations should consider putting the following in place:

1. *An intake form:* As discussed in an earlier chapter, an effective intake is essential for a smooth investigation. It is often helpful for managers and supervisors, when being trained or instructed on the taking of complaints, to be provided a form that helps them conduct the intake in the proper manner. Once that form is completed, it should be sent, either by fax or electronically, to whomever serves as the organizational clearinghouse on complaint management. This is usually a human resources professional but can also be counsel or other designated party. Once received, the party serving as the clearinghouse can respond with a simple acknowledgment, initiate a telephone consultation

to ensure proper handling occurs, or initiate a higher level intervention, such as an investigation. This transaction should then be documented on the intake form in the hands of the clearinghouse, and any follow-up noted by either the initiating party or the clearinghouse. The result is a solid record of the complaint and the action taken in response to the complaint. Because managers and supervisors recognize their liability if they are viewed as having ignored or failed to properly address certain complaints, they understand that forwarding the form provides them appropriate protection and corroboration that action was taken. An example of this type of form can be found in appendix A.

2. *Notices checklist:* There is a great deal of information to be transmitted at the outset of an interview, and therefore a great deal of information to be absorbed by the interviewee. In some cases, the information provided or not provided becomes a source of criticism of the investigation and its integrity. Subjects can claim that they were misled as to the purpose of the interview or were guaranteed confidentiality that was then not honored. For this reason, it is wise to create a "checklist" of notices to be reviewed with interviewees, and which they can take with them at the conclusion of the interview.

   This checklist should include a review of the purpose of the interview, conditions for sharing or not sharing information, instructions regarding reprisal, explanation of how notes will be used and retained, advice or instruction regarding discussion of the investigation or interview with others, and notice as to the possible consequences if it is determined that any party has violated policy. With a stable set of notices, investigators can practice reviewing the detailed information in a helpful and conversational way, and by asking interviewees to check or sign each item, help the interviewees focus on essential information. The signed version of the checklist should be retained in the investigative file and a blank form offered to the subject for his or her own records. In the case of telephone interviews, there should be an effort to transmit the document to the interviewee at the time the investigation is commenced and to receive a verbal affirmation of each item, which can then be recorded in the investigator's notes. An example of this type of checklist can be found in appendix B.

3.  *Cover or summary sheet:* Since investigations are generally concluded months or even years prior to the time discovery proceedings might call upon the investigator to recall them, a summary sheet can serve as an aid in recollection. A cover sheet should identify the complainant, witnesses, and respondents; and it should include a list of classes of evidence reviewed, such as "photographs of scene" and "complainant notes" (a detailed list itemizing all evidence reviewed should be included in the file), the period of time during which the investigation was conducted, and the date a report was issued verbally and/or in writing. Optionally, a brief summary of the allegations and findings can be incorporated into this summary sheet.

**Smart technology:** Increasingly, employees leave "electronic footprints" that become valuable evidence in investigations. E-mails, cell phone records, pager history, web forms, and instant and text messages are among the many types of records that are useful to investigators. Since these are generally produced and retained on employer-provided equipment, it is wise to plan for the discreet and prompt seizure of such records. Retrieving SIM cards, backing up e-mails sent and received to ensure they are not deleted from the system, capturing cookies and browser history, recovering data card records, and obtaining surveillance tapes where appropriate should be anticipated well in advance of a need to investigate. A person with expertise in information technology should be able to institute investigative data retrieval with a simple request from the appropriate authority, and at that point, electronic records should be frozen (made unalterable) and seized.

# CHAPTER 3

# Conducting the Intake

The process of "intake," or literally, *taking in the complaint*, is decidedly different from investigation. The quality of the intake will indisputably impact an investigator's ability to find facts.

Sepler & Associates' research has found a strong connection between how a complainant is treated when he or she makes the first complaint—to a supervisor, manager, HR staffer, compliance line, or other person—and whether he or she will ultimately bring a charge or lawsuit against the organization. Not surprisingly, charges of these types arise out of anger, frustration, and distrust in the organization's willingness to, interest in, or capability for managing the problem the employee has described. In essence, charges come when complainants believe they have not been listened to, have not been taken seriously, have been unfairly judged, or the organization has not been open and diligent. A charge is the weapon that a complainant has to tell his or her employer "if you won't listen to me, I will find someone to force you."

Assuming that organizations not only want to avoid lawsuits and charges but also would like real problems addressed, there is a strong imperative to provide solid training for those in a position to take a complaint. Focusing solely on investigative methodology and procedures and neglecting to ensure that intake is professional and consistent can undermine an organization's best intentions. Conflating intake and investigation appears to be one of the biggest errors an organization can make; the direct questioning and skepticism appropriate in certain investigative stages can crush complainants' confidence in their employer. The goal of an intake is to allow a person to be fully heard and their feelings affirmed.

Supervisors and managers are the most common participants in an intake, although human resources representatives and compliance staffs are commonly involved as well. They should be trained to recognize the difference between an employee expressing dissatisfaction or describing a simple conflict and allegations or intimations of policy violation (with the credo, that when in doubt, they should seek advice) in order to understand when it is important to escalate or at least seek advice about a matter. It can also be helpful to provide support and advice about reacting appropriately and in a timely manner to three different kinds of complaints, discussed below. Most importantly, the overall perspective on complaints by supervisors and managers should be managed.

Many view a complaint as a problem or a burden, and see complaining employees as making trouble or having ulterior motives. One of the best analogies for helping to alter this mindset is to point out that the longer an employee waits to raise an issue, the more organizational resources will be used to address it. Thus, if employees complain when they are merely troubled by something, it can often be addressed in a simple and straightforward manner. If, however, the employee waits until the matter is emotionally and psychologically unbearable (their "cup" is overflowing[1]), the organization could be substantially disrupted by investigations and charges. An early complaint (referred to below as a "contact") is really a gift—something being offered

---

[1] For a fuller understanding of this concept, see chapter 15, which describes the psychological dynamics of a complaint.

up voluntarily, even though the giver isn't obligated to do so. As such, managers and supervisors can be reminded that the proper etiquette when receiving a gift is to demonstrate gratitude and appreciation, thanking the employee and being appreciative of his or her giving the information.

Within the scope of complaints, managers and supervisors—and certainly human resources professionals—should be able to distinguish and prioritize among three common types of complaints. A summary of this "triage" categorization can be found in appendix C.

1. *The contact:* A contact is information brought forward by an employee as a result of the employee seeing, hearing, or learning about something he or she believes violates organizational rules or policies. It is usually a single event or incident, and generally the employee is not seeking help for him- or herself.

Following a regional meeting, Reginald stops in at the human resources office and speaks to Dave, a generalist. "Dave, I was in the sales meeting this morning, and one of the other reps made a real whopper of a racial joke. I can handle it, but I am sure there were some other people there who were really upset."

In the case of a contact, the employee reporting is rarely in a state of distress, so the primary interaction with the complainant is to thank him or her for bringing the information forward and obtain simple details about the meeting—when it was, who was present, whether this is the first incident the complainant is aware of, and so forth. In many such situations, a simple intervention can be orchestrated. The individual can be asked if he or she recalls telling the joke and coached to refrain from such behavior in the future, or a notice can be sent to all parties present at the meeting stating that issues have been raised about inappropriate humor and reviewing organizational policies with a warning that a recurrence could result in disciplinary action. The individual doing the intake, however, should never take such action in isolation. By consulting with the appropriate party (the clearinghouse) the proposed action can be affirmed and supported, or it can be overruled due to matters not recognized by the intake person. For instance, if it was determined that a senior manager was present when the behavior occurred, it might be important to determine whether that manager has already taken action (good) or failed to take steps to address it during or after the meeting (bad). What is important from a resource utilization perspective is that *many contact-type of complaints do not require and are not well served by a full investigation.*

2. *The concern:* A concern level complaint involves an employee who is experiencing some distress, whose psychological "cup" is fuller than he or she would like it to be and is attempting to seek relief. Ironically, it is quite usual in this case that although the person is seeking relief, he or she is still often convinced that reporting the matter would create more stress and not relieve it, so the person requests confidentiality and the opportunity to "just vent." The request will take the form of a statement that "I want to tell you about something, but I don't want you to do anything about it." What is happening psychologically is that he or she wants to "pour off" some stress so he or she can continue to cope. The serious dilemma here is that employers are not in a position to agree to keep secrets when it comes to possible violations of law and certain policies. Managers and supervisors and others in a position to receive complaints should be apprised of the importance of not promising inappropriate confidentiality, as well as how to handle the matter in a way that builds, rather than erodes, employee trust.

Yolanda has worked at your company for nearly 10 years, and over those years she has become very close to Jane, a supervisor in another department. They frequently have coffee together and discuss their work and personal lives in some detail. One day, Yolanda approaches Jane and says, "Jane, I need a friend. Can I discuss something with you in confidence?"

Jane pauses for a moment and says, "Yolanda, we are good friends, and I would like to instantly say yes, but the fact is that while in most circumstances I can honor that request, there are some circumstances under which I cannot. If you want to discuss something that might involve violations of our policy, I am under an obligation to be sure something is done about it, whether or not you and I would want it that way." Yolanda remains quiet, so Jane continues: "Of course, Yolanda, I care about whatever you have to say, and you know that I will do everything I can to help you and to preserve your privacy." Yolanda looks relieved, and tells Jane of an ongoing problem with her own supervisor.

A concern level complaint generally involves behavior that has continued over time—repeat or multiple incidents or ongoing conduct that is interfering with an employees' sense of comfort, well-being, or safety. The employee is probably still functioning well, although the employee issue triad might have begun to emerge (see p. 152). The most important steps in responding to an employee in this stage, in addition to the expression of gratitude, is to listen to whatever he or she wants to say, to recognize and validate his or her distress, and to provide as much information as possible regarding steps that will be taken to look into or address the issue. In these matters, the trust of the employee is fragile, and it is critical to not over-promise but diligently deliver on those promises made to keep the situation from escalating. It is also important to provide role clarification here to a person receiving the report; once he or she has referred the matter to the clearinghouse, he or she will have the ongoing responsibility to be a "process advocate" for the complainant—checking in regularly to ensure that the complainant feels fully informed of the process and that assurances and promises are kept. This does not mean there is substantive discussion about the complaint—generally there should not be—but real interest in the well-being for and understanding of the complainant. *Most concern level complaints will call for investigation, although some might only require the simplest of inquiries.*

3.  *The complaint:* A complaint level report is made by someone whose psychological "cup" is overflowing. The problematic behavior or situation has overshadowed all other aspects of the work environment. This individual is almost always reporting longstanding or highly explicit/offensive conduct and usually believes that the organization has condoned or allowed it since it has not been stopped in the past. The individual will have escalated emotions and may make ominous statements or excessive demands. He or she will often use legal terms to describe the problem they are having.

Three employees knock on the shift manager's door and burst in. "We need to speak to you," says Taye, the most senior of the employees. "We want to file a complaint about what's going on out on the floor. We think that there is a hostile environment here for people of color, and we have had enough of this. We are picked on, disrespected, and discriminated against, and no one here gives a damn—"

"Whoa," interrupts the shift manager, "why don't you calm down and have a seat?"

"We don't need a seat. We don't need to calm down. We need those supervisors fired today," responds Taye.

In a complaint, the tendency of a manager or supervisor

might be to become defensive or upset, or to try to encourage employees to "be reasonable." These responses are ineffective at best and inflammatory at worst. Those who do intake should expect and accept a high degree of emotion during this kind of complaint, and not take it personally; nor should he or she expect that the initial version of events will be factually accurate. In fact, in this type of intake, one should expect to hear "advocacy speak," a term that recognizes that people in distress are much more interested in telling "their side" than a neutral recitation of the facts. Thus, the term refers to the expression of feelings and events for purposes of persuading and accomplishing an alliance, supportive response, or other emotional validation of the event or events being described. People doing intake can recognize this and accept that first reports of this intensity will routinely include distortions, magnifications, overstatements, omissions, and outright misstatements of fact.

Attempts to instruct complainants to "stick to the facts" or to be reasonable simply will escalate the intensity of this phenomenon. Rather, as experienced investigators understand, this type of overstatement is a routine and essential part of processing of events that is best managed by validating the emotions or feelings being expressed ("I can see that you are really upset.") until the complainants have exhausted what they want to say.

The hallmark of responding to complaint level reports is to avoid defensiveness and to emphasize promptness and action. Telling the complainants that you take their concern very seriously, and instituting immediate interim actions to minimize further disruption and to secure evidence (i.e., separating parties, securing documents) while being very specific and precise about next steps is essential. What is most essential is that the urgency of the complaint, as indicated by the distress of the complainant, is communicated to the clearinghouse to orchestrate a proper response.

No matter the stage, the intake should not involve interrogation or deep fact-finding. It is a preliminary, separate and distinct stage of complaint handling that sets the stage for the appropriate designation of resources and effective identification and resolution of issues.

In summary, intake should involve the following:

- Thanking the person for coming forward and being willing to describe his or her concerns.
- Listening attentively to what the person has to say.
- Avoiding interrupting, expressing doubt, or challenging the version provided.
- Determining the impact the complainant believes the situation or conduct is currently having and taking immediate steps to neutralize or counter it, where possible. (This also may mean acting to preserve evidence or protect others, depending on the severity of allegations.)
- Being appropriately empathetic, acknowledging the very real feelings being expressed but not validating any facts.
- Describing in detail steps that will be taken to pursue the matter. Will this matter be referred elsewhere? When, and what will happen next? Will there be an investigation? What will the complainant be expected to do?
- Expressing concern for the well-being of the complainant and describing prohibitions against reprisal.
- Getting the basics—and only the basics—from the complainant:
  - What happened?
  - Who was involved?
  - Where and when?
  - Was this the first time or were there similar events prior?
  - Who saw it? Who may have heard it or seen something?
  - Who did you tell about it? When?
  - What actions did you take?

- ◆ Do you have any electronic or written records that would be helpful in understanding or verifying this event?
- ◆ What prompted this report?

The intake *should not* include:

- ■ Extensive or intensive note-taking. (A preprinted intake form can be very helpful.)
- ■ Detailed questioning.
- ■ Pressing for details or challenging versions of events.
- ■ Questions or comments about the character of the complainant or any other employee.
- ■ Statements as to whether the person doing the intake believes what he or she is hearing.
- ■ Asking the complainant what he or she did to create the situation. ("What was your part in it?" may be the worst question one can ask in this situation.)
- ■ Trying to "trick" the complainant into a retraction.
- ■ Labeling the complainant as a "whiner."
- ■ Implying that a "false complaint" could result in problems for the complainant, or making veiled statements about the reputation of any accused.

Once the intake is complete, the organizational clearinghouse process should be used to determine if and what type of investigation is needed (i.e., if everything the complainant has alleged is true, would it be a violation of policy? Are there facts that cannot be independently verified?) and the investigative intake should commence. By increasing organizational competence and role clarity regarding intake versus investigation, organizations predict a greater perception of fairness by employees, a lower rate of litigated matters, and a higher degree of cooperation when and if an investigation does begin.

# CHAPTER 4

# The Decision to Conduct an Investigation

In reviewing all of the purposes of an investigation as described in chapter 2, each organization must examine a complaint and determine whether an investigation is appropriate. In some cases, full investigations are begun with little thought as to their necessity. If the allegations are not extremely serious, there should be consideration as to whether a coaching approach might be sufficient absent a fact-finding. If the determination is that the current allegation might be an indicator of a more serious set of behaviors or circumstances, this should be considered as well. Sometimes a simple admission comes as the result of an informal inquiry by a supervisor or manager, in which case an investigation is unnecessary. The following are a set of questions that can assist a clearinghouse to decide the appropriate level of investigation or intervention:

1. If everything that has been alleged is true, would the organization take disciplinary action? If everything that has been alleged is true, would the organization take remedial or educational action?
2. Are there actual disputes about fact at this time?
3. Has there been prior, similar conduct involving these individuals or this organization?

4. Is it necessary to know the facts in order to respond to this situation (i.e., complaint involves an employee who no longer works for the organization)?
5. Does the current complaint suggest a larger, undiscovered issue, problem, or situation?
6. Are there multiple complainants?
7. Is the accused an agent of the organization?

Once a decision has been made to conduct an investigation, the clearinghouse should ensure that the person who will do the investigation is the appropriate person to be doing so.

**Neutrality:** An investigator must appear to be—and actually be—neutral. This means that prior relationships with any of the parties should be carefully considered. An adverse or problematic relationship—or a close or friendly relationship—to a party can be a barrier to neutrality. To the extent that prior relationships exist but are deemed to not interfere with the neutrality of the investigator, it is well worth considering asking parties at the outset of each interview, "Do you have any reason to believe that I cannot be neutral in this matter?" and to capture and consider their response

**Time:** Timeliness is one of the great challenges of employment investigations. Although there appears to be some tolerance for investigations that are lengthy[1], it is advisable to strive for prompt and efficient investigations, and to avoid investigations that drag on for months because of investigator workload. The complexity of the allegations

---

[1] In *Tatum v. Arkansas Dep't of Health* (8th Cir. 6/20/05), the court stated that the complainant "contends that (her employer) failed to take her complaint seriously because of the amount of time it took to complete the investigation. (The complainant) presented evidence that the investigation was not begun until two weeks after her complaint and took eight weeks to complete.... While we do not fully endorse the handling of (the complaint) we do not find the investigation falls below the required standard." The court went on to explain its reasoning and particularly to point out that there was no further harassment during the investigation period. See also *Swenson v. Potter*, 271 F.3d at 1184,1192 (9th Cir 2001)

should be considered in the selection of an investigator. Making sure an investigator can devote adequate time and attention is a key factor in assigning cases.

**Skill:** Not every investigator is as skilled and experienced as any other. In cases likely to be litigated, the most skilled and experienced investigators are the most qualified to conduct the investigation. More than that, however, a good clearinghouse recognizes the varied styles and skills of each investigator. Perhaps some are particularly good with blue-collar workers, while others excel at investigations involving executives. Choosing an investigator the same race or gender as the complainant or respondent may be a strategic choice to encourage cooperation.[2] Furthermore, if the organization assigns two investigators to each case, pairing investigators of different or similar styles should be a deliberate decision, and of course, pairing more skilled and experienced with those still learning can be valuable for the organization.

**Internal or external?** The decision about whether to keep an investigation in-house or to bring in an external investigator is a complex decision involving allocation of resources, profile of the investigation, honoring internal expertise, considering the difficulty one might encounter with decision-makers, and simple capacity. Although operational factors are unique to each organization, sometimes it is the character of the claim or charge that should drive the decision as to whether an internal investigator is needed. The chart on the following page provides a simple test to help in the decision whether to conduct the investigation internally or to bring in outside help.

---

[2] In Sepler & Associates' research, interviewees did not express different levels of satisfaction based on the gender, race, or age of the investigator, with the exception of feeling more satisfied with same-race investigators in racial discrimination and harassment complaints.

| Look at the matter | 1 point | 2 points | 3 points |
|---|---|---|---|
| The matter to be investigated is | Simple, involving two parties and one or two incidents | Moderate in complexity, involving more than two parties or multiple incidents | High in complexity, involving multiple parties and multiple incidents, or allegations of hostile environment |
| The person(s) accused of misconduct | Are non-managerial and at the same rank as the complainant | Are middle management and higher in rank than the complainant | Are senior managers or executives |
| The complaints involve | Inappropriate language, jokes, or simple misconduct | A combination of inappropriate language and multiple acts of misconduct | Extreme racial, sexual, or threatening/harassing behavior |
| The person to do the investigating | Is extremely experienced and confident | Has some experience, but is uncertain about the best way to proceed | Is inexperienced or is in a reporting relationship to a party in the investigation |

1–4 Almost certainly manageable internally
5–9 Consider using outside investigator
10 Recommend outside investigator

# CHAPTER 5

# The Heart of an Investigation – Conducting the Investigative Interview

An investigation is only as good as the quality of the information that is gathered. The primary information gathering mechanism in an investigation is an interview. It is the way we find out what people have experienced, perceived, and felt. The interview gives the investigator an opportunity to pay full attention to someone in order to understand them and to observe them. A good interview is well orchestrated and scrupulously managed, while at the same time appearing to be relaxed and spontaneous. Everything from the setting of the interview to the pre-interview chatter lends itself to the effectiveness of the interview process. The term "process" reflects the fact that many things are occurring during what might appear to be a simple question-and-answer session:

- The investigator is attempting to ascertain facts.
- The investigator is attempting to assess the credibility of the parties.
- The investigator is attempting to generate credibility and faith in the process.
- The investigator is attempting to create trust, where appropriate.

■ The investigator is attempting to provide those accused with an opportunity to fully respond.

It is critical to keep in mind that the purpose of an investigative interview is to get information that is accurate. In some cases, this is simply a matter of listening to someone; in others, it is about asking the right questions. In still others, it is about persuading people to disclose or describe things that are against their own interests or that they don't want you to know. Although there are many schools of thought about interviewing techniques, it must be said that employment investigations are distinctly different from criminal investigations.

Those familiar with harsh techniques sometimes used in the latter are well advised to ensure that they have a broad array of techniques at their disposal to achieve investigative goals. Only a small percentage of those people interviewed in employment investigations are subsequently terminated or resign as a result. This means that the people being interviewed will continue to be employed by the employer that is now questioning them. In most cases, there is very little interest on an employer's part in alienating or demeaning an employee. Rather, employers seek continuing engagement from their employees, even those who may have behaved poorly. Although strong-arm techniques and intense adversarial interrogation might "get the job done" on a particular day, they do not serve the long-term needs of an employment situation and should be avoided in less-than-emergent situations. Therefore, it is worthwhile to determine those things that are decidedly *not* the purpose of an investigative interview process:

■ The investigator is not attempting to create a tactical or strategic advantage.
■ The investigator is not attempting to "create a record" as one would in a deposition.
■ The investigator is not attempting to "trick" people or to manipulate the intention of the interviewee.

Although every interview is different, and there are decidedly different strategies to be used in various types of interviews, all effective interviews have five distinct stages. These stages are specific and specifically ordered, and "skipping" a step for any reason significantly diminishes the productivity and integrity of the interview.

## Stage 1 – opening and tone setting

Just as a real estate agent "stages" a home for sale, an investigator must set the stage for the interview. An interview begins as soon as a subject is contacted to be interviewed. The investigator should prepare a "script" for notifying interviewees about interviews, especially if they are being arranged by someone other than the investigator him- or herself. This will be the first opportunity to set the tone with the interviewee, so the investigator must decide how the notification will occur and what will be said.

It is critical that the notice, or "invitation," conveys the professionalism and neutrality that will ensure him or her of the discretion and care the investigator will take. Some investigators introduce themselves as "consultants," rather than using the term "investigator." Some use formal language to impress upon the subjects the importance of the meeting, while others use decidedly casual language to avoid generating anxiety or hyper-vigilance. As with all other aspects of an investigation, consistency in the information people are given prior to their interview is important.

Part of the staging of an interview is the careful preparation the investigator must undertake. The preparation should be rigorous but not confining. In a complainant interview, the investigator will no doubt have some information about the nature of the complaint from the intake. It is, however, essential that the investigator consider the complainant interview an interview *de novo* and not focus only on what was communicated during the intake. The intake information should serve to suggest areas of questioning, but generally it is inadvisable for an investigator to prepare detailed fact questions for a complainant interview.

In the case of witnesses and respondents, the investigator should be prepared for the interview by carefully identifying areas that he or she wants to explore with the interviewee, and perhaps by identifying specific questions that will need to be asked. But if it is too carefully scripted, an interview may fail to explore areas that can emerge during the discourse or adapt questioning based on the demeanor or language of the interviewee. An interviewer with an intimate familiarity of information already gathered and a clear intention of interviewing a specific witness or respondent will net the most productive and structurally sound interview.

The investigator must also be familiar with the organizational policies and procedures governing the interview. Interviewees may ask the consequences of declining to be interviewed or may ask to have a union representative present. Interviewees are often concerned about the specific procedures that will be used to review findings. Although external investigators cannot always anticipate every question about internal operations, it is to be expected that they will have worked with the organization to prepare to respond to questions regarding requirements, procedures, and timing of the investigation. The pre-interview checklist (see chapter 2) can be helpful in this regard, provided it is customized for each investigation and each organization.

The investigator should choose a neutral setting for an interview whenever possible. This should be a well-ventilated, well-lit space with restrooms and a copy machine nearby. The room should be private, both in the respect that parties to the interview will not be able to see one another coming and going, and audibly and visually private; cubicles and windowed offices should be avoided.

Room configuration plays a significant role in the dynamics of an interview. Sitting across a table from an interviewee creates an unnecessary physical barrier and is less desirable than sitting kitty-corner at a table. This setting allows the investigator to more fully observe the body language of the interviewee but does not create a sense of vulnerability for the interviewee. The investigator should prepare his or her space by having all necessary paperwork arranged, note-taking apparatus prepared, and several empty file folders for the collection of documents. A pitcher of water and several cups are a good idea. If the room contains computers or other monitors, they should be turned off; any other distracting items or displays should be removed. The goal is to create an environment in which one can fully concentrate without undue distraction or discomfort.

The most significant aspect of the first stage of interviewing is the demeanor of the interviewer. Although the expectations of the interviewee will vary widely, the goal of the first 5 to 10 minutes of an interview is going to be the same: to humanize the process. Whether an interview subject is anxious, worried, excited, or angry, treating him or her in a reasonable way and connecting on a human level will pay off in a variety of ways. When the interviewee arrives for the interview, everything should be properly arranged so that the investigator can give the interviewee his or her undivided attention. The interviewer should be welcoming, professional, neutral, and active. Offering the person a drink of water, assisting in hanging his or her coat, gesturing toward a chair, and inquiring whether the temperature of the room is appropriate are all ways to demonstrate an interest and willingness to engage the interview subject.

Although some subjects arrive clearly unhappy to be summoned, most will be cooperative. This spirit of cooperation should be nurtured by engaging in informal conversation or by asking easily answerable questions—including inane questions about the weather, if necessary. To the extent that an investigator can get a bit of a dialogue occurring with the interview subject, it provides an opportunity to observe their demeanor, tone of voice, speed of communication, any nonverbal "tics" or habits, and other communicative idiosyncrasies in a relatively unstressed state. These observations (called *baseline observations*) can be very helpful in assessing credibility, and they also allow the interviewer to make adjustments in speed and tone of questioning and grammatical construction.

Specific baseline observations may include the following:

- What processing speed is evident? Does the person pause before answering questions or respond immediately?
- Is the person reserved or spontaneously forthcoming?
- How much detail does the person automatically provide?
- How does the person respond to questions about details? Is he or she highly observant?
- Is the person facially expressive?
- Is the person animated? Still?
- What is the nature of the person's eye contact?
- What can you observe about the speed of speech?
- Does the person display a strong vocabulary or are there limitations?
- What is the volume the person speaks at in normal conversation?
- Can you identify the cadence of the person's speech?
- What level of nonverbal communication is typical for this person? Does he or she use hand gestures when speaking? Roll his or her eyes? Tap impatiently?

To make these observations, the investigator should set a tone of two-way discussion in the first part of the interview. Since this will include welcoming the person, asking questions such as "Did you have any problem finding this room? Or "How was the traffic today?" can be sufficient to begin that conversation. It is also appropriate to ask logistical questions: "What limits do you have on your time?" "Are you comfortable that your desk is covered for as long as we will need, or will you need to check back?"

An interview subject who arrives angry or expresses hostility should be handled with care. Allow or invite the interviewee to express his or her concerns and respond respectfully and with empathy.

> "If what you say is true, and this is the fourth time you have been asked to discuss this incident, I can understand your frustration. Let's be sure to be extremely thorough so this is the absolute last time you get asked the same questions."

> "I can tell that you are unhappy at the moment. Do you want to tell me what's going on?"

> "I am sure this is a difficult and frightening time for you. Being accused of misconduct is a scary thing. The good thing is that this process is designed to be sure you have a chance to respond to each and every allegation made against you, and to help identify others who might have information I need to be sure this process is completely fair. Let's go through this checklist, which describes the 'ground rules' I follow, and see if that addresses some of your concerns."

> "I recognize that you don't want to answer any questions, and I certainly can't force you to, but let's talk about what happens if you do and you don't cooperate...."

Absent strong resistance, as above, the goal should be to keep the first few moments of the interview relatively low-key. As the informal "chitchat" abates, the investigator must make a quick assessment of what the interviewee knows about the matter under investigation. Generally, that can be done by beginning the introduction to the process with the question, "What do you know about why you are here?" In some cases, the person will be absolutely certain of the subject to be discussed, and in other cases, he or she will have no idea. The investigator will need to base the introduction of the process, in part, on the interviewee's response.

"Frank, I'd like to explain how we're going to proceed in here, but first, let me ask you what you know about why we're here today."

"Susan, I'm aware that you contacted Mary Jones in human resources and asked to speak with me as part of an ongoing investigation. Can you tell me what you know about the subject of this investigation?"

If the subject denies any knowledge about the subject of the interview, the investigator should tell the person he or she is being interviewed as part of an investigation. The person should also be told whether he or she is there as a witness or as a respondent. If the person correctly identifies the subject of the interview or the nature of the complaint, the investigator can inquire as to whether he or she would like to retrieve any documents, calendars, and so forth that would be helpful. Once that is done, it will be necessary to review the "ground rules" for the discussion. The tone should remain conversational and comfortable. At this point, the interviewee should be provided a copy of the pre-interview checklist, and the interview should commence.

The investigator should be familiar with the pre-interview checklist and find a way to introduce the checklist that demonstrates reviewing it is for the benefit of the interviewee.

"Sarah, I appreciate your coming to see me. I am sure you have a lot of questions about why we're here. This checklist will help to familiarize you with who I am and what I'm doing, and also to make sure that you fully understand this process and your role in it. I want to be certain that the people I interview are well informed about their obligations and their protections, so we're going to take whatever time is necessary to go over this. The first thing this list says is that I am conducting an investigation into possible misconduct in the widget division. Do you see that? The next thing you'll see is that it says it is my job to be neutral.

This means I am not on anyone's side; I am not representing anyone, and I am not an advocate. I am prepared to find out what happened regardless of who it makes look good or bad. Does that make sense to you? Do you have any concerns about my ability to be neutral?"

The review of the checklist is also a chance for the investigator to exhibit professionalism and a capacity for listening, and to establish rapport with the interviewee. The review should never be droning or robotic but animated and interesting.

Once the checklist has been reviewed, initialed, and other logistical matters have been settled, the first stage is nearly complete, and the actual questioning should begin. *The first 2 to 10 questions an interviewer asks should be neutral, easily answerable, and generally unrelated to the investigation itself.* These questions generally include:

- Can you tell me your full name?
- How long have you worked here?
- Where did you work before this?
- What is your position?
- How long have you been in this position?
- Can you give be a brief summary of your duties?
- Do you get feedback on your performance? What has that feedback been?
- Have you been promoted? Demoted? Disciplined? Gotten recognition?

Clearly, the investigator could easily answer these questions via a cursory review of the subject's personnel file, so his or her purpose is not to acquire information. It is to give the interviewee an opportunity to be forthcoming. These questions, about which only a very few people would feel a need to fabricate, create a positive and successful tone for the interview. It allows the interviewer to continue to get a sense of what tone and rhythm to set, and will generally relax a nervous interviewee. The tone an interviewer is striving for is cooperation and agreeability, and if successful it gives the interviewee the experience of "succeeding" in the interview. Once several of these questions have been asked, and the interview subject appears to be engaging in the conversation, the interview can begin the second phase.

# Stage 2 — uninterrupted initial narrative

An investigative interview aspires to understand the perspective of the person being interviewed. One can only truly gain that perspective by allowing the person to share it without the bias or influence of specific inquiries or instructions. By allowing an interviewee to share his or her "story" with the least interruption possible, several things are accomplished: The interviewee's mental organization of events improves, and his or her memory gets jogged; the interviewer may hear information that provides new insights, perspectives, or areas of inquiry that would not be apparent were one to immediately ask questions; and it gives the interviewee a firm sense of being listened to rather than guided or manipulated.

The uninterrupted initial narrative is most important and likely most lengthy in the interviews of complainants and respondents, but despite its likely shortened state, is just as relevant and important in witness interviews. The objective is to have the interview subject describe things in their own words with the least amount of prompting necessary. Thus, for complainants, initiating this stage may be facilitated by simply saying, "Why don't you tell me why you are here." Or "Tell me what has been going on." For witnesses and respondents, interviewers will need to use progressively specific questions to reach a point where "storytelling" begins. For instance,

> "Do you know why we're here today?"
> "I think I do."
> "Why don't you tell me what you know about why we're here."

"I think this is about what happened with Kalid and Kiera."

"Are you familiar with that situation?"

"Sort of."

"Why don't you tell me what you know."

Or:

"Lisa, as I told you earlier, there have been some concerns raised about your interactions with some of your coworkers. Have you been made aware of their concerns?"

"No one has said anything to me."

"Well, let's see what we can do to get to the bottom of those concerns. Do you recall attending a conference in Omaha last year?"

"Yes."

"Do you recall any events in Omaha that might have given rise to some concerns?"

"I have no idea."

"Well, Lisa, it appears that some of the issues we will be discussing here began to emerge during an evening cocktail hour. Do you remember attending a cocktail hour?"

"Yes."

"Do you recall any discussion or events during the cocktail hour that might have given rise to concerns?"

"I don't remember."

"Do you recall having an argument with two of your coworkers during that cocktail hour?"

"Yes."

"Why don't you tell me what you remember about that."

Whatever strategy is used to get a person talking, it is important to remember that the goal of this stage is an *uninterrupted* narrative. It is a time for the interviewer to carefully observe and to listen to the entire "arc" of the story, from beginning to end with as little intervention as possible. The interviewer will certainly formulate questions, but this is not the time to interrupt or slow the flow of information with questions; rather it is time to encourage continued descriptive verbalization.

During the uninterrupted initial narrative, the interviewer should demonstrate interest and enthusiasm, probing only when absolutely necessary. Appreciative prompts, such as "Mm-hmm," or asking "And then what happened?" are helpful. Although some note-taking will be helpful at this stage to ensure that key points are noted and to remind the interviewer of questions he or she may ask later, this is not the time to attempt detailed or verbatim notes. In fact, taking only minimal notes provides the interviewee with permission to revisit information already shared, to revise or correct information, and to be chronologically a bit disorganized. This is part of the "mental housekeeping" that will be helpful when, in the third stage, the interviewer will be probing deeply into details.

The interviewer should be generously empathetic, acknowledging emotion and encouraging individuals to describe things fully.

> "I know this is hard for you, but it is really valuable for me to hear what you have to say."

> "I can certainly understand, if what you are describing happened, how difficult that might have been.

The art of investigative empathy is to be responsive and *to acknowledge feelings without appearing to validate a particular version of events.* Remember, too, that much of what might emerge in a first telling of events might be "advocacy speak." By acknowledging the feelings, the investigator is moving the subject along a continuum from "telling my side" to "describing the facts."

For those who believe interviewing is about asking the right questions, this stage can be frustrating. To an uninformed observer, the interviewer appears passive, and some interviewees can prattle on for long periods of time.

Tolerating disorganization and being patient are investigative skills. It is important to see this stage as an essential precursor to active inquiry, both from the standpoint of gaining a full understanding of the situation and from the standpoint of accommodating human recall and emotion. It is helpful to understand that orchestrating this "storytelling" stage is anything but passive and will greatly enrich the investigator's ability to ask good questions and assess the credibility of the interviewee.

The uninterrupted narrative will be complete when the answer to "Is there any other information you can give me about this situation/event/behavior/relationship?" is "No." For respondents, this will need to be the response for each area of inquiry; for witnesses, the question might be phrased, "Have you told me everything you know about...?" When the story has been fully told, it is time to move on to the third stage of the investigative interview.

## Stage 3 — reconstruction

Once the interviewer has heard the "story" and knows the general themes and subject areas, the next stage is to visit every part of the narrative again to obtain the most detailed information possible. To create a transition, the investigator will generally thank the interviewee for being forthcoming and for his or her thoroughness, and explain that the interviewer would now like to go back through what the interviewee has said and ask clarifying questions. The tone and spirit of this statement should be cooperative, including enlisting the aid of the interviewee in ensuring that the investigator has a completely accurate and detailed understanding of what has happened. This is a good time for the investigator to take a brief break, to organize his or her questions, and to craft a "game plan" for going forward.

The questioning should focus on a specific aspect of the allegations and move forward in a logical and coherent manner. For this reason, many investigators choose to proceed chronologically.

"Let's start with the very first time you realized there was an issue. Was that when you were working the night shift?"

Assuming the response to the above is in the affirmative, the next question would be "What date exactly was it?" followed by "Was anyone else present?" and so forth.

Some investigators prefer a "reverse chronology," beginning with most recent events and moving backward; others try to focus on what they consider to be the most significant or serious events, moving toward the less significant. Each matter calls for a consideration of the sequence that will result in the interviewee's continuing to be cooperative and forthcoming.

Minimally, of course, the goal is to have the who, what, where, when, and how for each incident. The following questions are usually appropriate, with specific probes then dependent on the unique set of facts:

- What exactly happened?
- Where did it happen?
- When did it happen?
- Who saw it? Who heard it?
- Who did you tell about it?
- Who else knows about it? How do they know?
- What did you do in response?
- What other actions were taken?
- Are you aware of other, similar events or behavior?
- What happened immediately afterward?
- Did you make any notes, diary entries, or other record of this?
- Have you had any written correspondence about this?
- Did you save (physical item)? Where is it now?
- Are there additional things I should know about this issue/situation/event?

The investigator should enlist the active cooperation of the interviewee by encouraging him or her to "fill in the blanks" of earlier statements. In complex or longstanding situations, the interviewer might choose to create a chronology on a white board or flipchart and invite the interviewee to make notations or help to organize it to ensure that there is clarity in the interviewer's understanding. The interviewer can also ask the subject to demonstrate actions that might be unclear or ambiguous in the telling.

> "When you say that he 'leaned up on you,' what does that mean exactly?"
>
> "He would come up behind me and put his elbows on my shoulders."
>
> "I need to be clearer on this. [Places chair in an open area] Let's have the chair be you, and you show me exactly how he approached you...."

The investigator should not hesitate to ask the interviewee to draw diagrams or even to jointly visit an area where something transpired to ensure that the investigator has the best possible picture of what is happening. This is also the stage where acquiring evidence is essential. (See chapter 10 for a detailed discussion of identifying and acquiring evidence.)

The third stage of the investigative interview is less emotional and more analytical than the prior two stages. Having reacted appropriately and demonstrated understanding, the interviewer can now feel free to conduct an "all business" interview with as many open-ended and specific questions as he or she feels necessary to gather the full facts. Similarly, the interviewer can now take detailed notes and even ask the interview subject to repeat responses to ensure the accuracy of those notes.

One thing investigators should pay attention to is the momentum of an interview. A successful interview is almost like a dance; there is a focus and rhythm between questioner and responder that becomes more satisfying to both as the interview progresses. The investigator is able to respond to the interview subject in a manner that creates more energy for the next response, and so on. This occurs when an investigator is highly sensitive to tone, rhythm, and timing, and uses all of the tools at his or her disposal to "match" pace, rhythm, tone, and inflection with the interviewee. In the third stage, in the best of all circumstances, the witness is placing a large amount of effort into assuring that the information in the notes of the investigator is thorough and accurate. Using responses such as "Excellent," or "That is extremely helpful" as facts are reviewed help to promote this cooperative give-and-take.

If the second stage of the interview might appear to be inactive, this stage can be tedious, particularly if there are multiple incidents to be reviewed. The investigator should be mindful of the interviewee's mental fatigue (as well as his or her own!), and pause for breaks or meals. It is important to never rush this stage and to carefully explore each and every aspect of the matter being investigated.

During this stage, the investigator may encounter inconsistencies or may formulate theories about the truthfulness of the interviewee. Certain facts may not hang together, or the version of events may have changed over the course of reviewing them. If this happens, credibility notations can and should be *made separate from the investigator's notes,* but confrontations or inquiries about those inconsistencies or impressions should not be communicated until all detailed inquiry is done and the interview has progressed into stage four.

## Stage 4—deconstruction/push

The most challenging part of any interview is the necessary sea change that occurs in the fourth stage. Up until now, the interviewer must work very hard to build a rapport with the interviewee. Cooperation and empathy are two of the tools that are most helpful in this regard. Once all of the information that is needed is "in the can," the interviewer must now identify steps necessary to test or question the accuracy or validity of the facts. Some of the things to be explored in this stage are areas where the subject appeared evasive; questions or areas of discussion in which the interviewer made observations of the interviewee's demeanor straying off the "baseline" observations; inconsistencies or gaps in recollection; versions of events that differ from those of others; improbable events or sequences of events; and the presentation of evidence that impeaches or challenges the veracity of the interviewee.

It is critically important that the deconstructive stage of the interview move from least to most confrontational, as serious confrontations can cause the interviewee to disengage or even leave the interview. This will certainly diminish the trust the interviewee may have developed for the interviewer.

The method for confronting inconsistencies or differing versions of events may be low-key, and can include the investigator's suggestion that it is his or her own recollection that may be faulty as opposed to the interviewee's version of events.

"I have a question about the incident you're described happening in the elevator. When you were first describing it to me, I was sure you said it was last Tuesday, but when we discussed it in detail, you said it was a few months ago. Am I confused?"

"Hmm...maybe you can help me out here. It seems like you told me you were too afraid to tell anyone about what happened, but then later on you indicated you had complained to your supervisor about the situation. Can you help me clarify?"

"I appreciate your going into so much detail in explaining what happened. Can you help me understand why Fred might have said that, in fact, you called him, rather than vice versa?"

In the latter case, it is important to observe the interviewee as the investigator presents Fred's version. Is there a momentary disorientation? Does the interviewee appear to make a calm assessment of the differing version? Does she backpedal? Does she immediately deny Fred's version or offer proof of her own? These are important clues to help the investigator gain an impression of the interviewee's credibility. Dealing with denials will be discussed further in the section on special issues in interviewing the respondent but also may apply to techniques useful in a second "responsive" interview with a complainant (an interview responsive to the respondent's interview).

As the type of confrontation becomes more direct, it is important for the investigator to remember his or her purpose, which is to neutrally gather facts. An admission of wrongdoing provides certainty, but it should not be considered a "success" any more than a sincere denial is. Remember too that it is in the interest of employers to treat all employees with dignity and respect, even those who may have violated rules or policy. Direct confrontations with contradictory evidence or statements should be handled routinely and neutrally. Admissions or denials should be explored but not beyond a professional or reasonable point.

The investigator should always keep a temperate tone of voice, speaking slowly and calmly, and maintaining reasonable eye contact and body language. Reinforce the importance of truthfulness and cooperation, rather than allude to discipline or consequences.

In the case of evidence, such as documents that directly contradict the statement of an interviewee, the method of confrontation might be simply to introduce the evidence or source of information and confirm his or her familiarity with the document or person who provided it, give him or her a chance to read or review it, and to ask for a response, reaction, or explanation. The investigator appropriately makes credibility observations during this transaction to note obvious expressions of dissembling, surprise, or confusion.

More information to support this part of the interview can be found in chapter 9.

# Stage 5 — closing

Closing the interview involves confirmation of all of the information gathered, and providing a space in time for the interviewee to re-engage in the process. The investigator should inform the subject that he or she has completed the necessary questioning for the time being, and that it is now necessary to ensure that all of the information gathered has been accurate. This means going back through the investigator's notes to confirm what has been described and the details provided. If the interviewee disagrees with the interviewer's description of events, the additions or alterations should be noted as "stage five corrections," rather than altering the notes. The investigator will need to decide whether the new versions are credible and simply clarify prior versions, or whether there has been a change in factual recollection and whether this appears self-serving.

The closing is also a time to restate the "ground rules" with the subject of the interview—instructing him or her not to discuss the interview with others, review the prohibition against reprisal, and explain the next steps in the investigation. It should also ensure that the interviewee has appropriate expectations about the information he or she is entitled to as the investigation goes forward.

In some cases, an interviewee will be sufficiently upset or angry at the end of an interview that the investigator may believe arrangements should be made for the individual to be placed on leave or allowed to depart for the rest of the workday. This contingency should have been considered in advance and appropriate steps taken to offer such an arrangement to the interviewee as part of the planning process (see chapter 6).

If, during the interview, evidence was identified and not provided, it is important that the interviewer review expectations for evidence delivery, and establish a plan for retrieval of whatever documents or other evidence the witness has agreed to provide.

Finally, each interviewee should leave with a full understanding that he or she may be called upon again should it be necessary, and they should be provided with a means of contacting the investigator should he or she recall further information or think of others who might be helpful for the investigator to speak with.

# CHAPTER 6

# Planning the Investigation

After conducting the preliminary interview with the complainant, the investigator must pause and plan. "Diving in" to a series of interviews and inquiries may be tempting, but often works against the prospect of an efficient and effective interview process. For those newer to investigations, planning the investigation can be done with the assistance of more experienced investigators. For more experienced investigators, demonstrating thoughtfulness in planning provides assurance that the matter at hand is not being routinized and a good deal of thought has been invested in the planning.

The following steps are recommended as part of investigative planning.

## Interim actions

Once the allegations are fully understood, the employer might need to take interim actions to ensure that the work environment is most conducive to an investigation uncomplicated by allegations of reprisal or new allegations involving the same parties. Consider whether interim actions to remove or separate parties are appropriate. This might include offering paid leave to a distressed complainant, placing alleged bad actors on leave, issuing instructions to supervisors to assign parties to different work areas, temporarily assigning workers to separate shifts, or instructing parties to minimize contact. In addition, the employer should take interim actions to preserve evidence and provide for the safety and stability of the work environment.

Data that will be reviewed in the investigation, such as financial records, sign-in sheets, personnel files, transcripts, and security records, should be sealed to avoid tampering or alterations. In cases where allegations involve alleged electronic communications such as e-mail, the ability of parties to alter those systems should be minimized by freezing access or immediate backup of records. If there are concerns about the physical safety of the work environment, appropriate steps should be taken to ensure that proper supervision and security is provided.

## Establishing scope

Investigations are, in many ways, like a boat journey down a river. One hopes for smooth water, but occasionally the unexpected occurs. There is the lure exploring attractive tributaries, but going down those lesser paths can also result in becoming stranded, having lost sight of the original objective. Inexperienced investigators are most often hampered not by the decision of what or when to ask but by a lack of clarity and focus in investigative scope. One can observe the gradual loss of clarity, and at times, the loss of control of the investigation as the scope of inquiry becomes muddier or wider.

The scope of an investigation is determined once a decision has been made to investigate a claim. An investigation is necessary when combinations of the following occur:

- The claim alleges that policies have been violated and/or the claim alleges that law has been violated.
- The employer would likely take remedial or punitive action if the allegations were true.
- There is a likelihood or possibility that the claims

are part of a pattern of conduct or represent a widespread set of behaviors.

■ There is a dispute about what has transpired or a variety of perspectives about what has transpired.

The scope of an investigation should be established by examining those allegations—currently known and those that emerge in the future—that represent a potential violation of policies or work rules.

In the case of harassment and discrimination claims, the investigator must make a specific decision as to whether claims of unrelated, but potentially actionable, misconduct will be incorporated into the current investigation or whether they should be investigated separately. In the case of independent or neutral investigators, this may need to be clarified in writing as an amendment to the retention letter.

Jane Smith, an employee of the Redi-Set Printing Company, has alleged that Jack Dawson, a press foreman, has been isolating her and attempting to kiss and touch her. She reports that she has complained to her supervisor, who she alleges responded by stating that Dawson "does that to all of the pretty girls." Smith states that her supervisor added that Dawson "robs the company blind," but everyone is too afraid of him to do anything about it.

In this particular case, Smith has made a specific allegation which, if true, would likely violate Redi-Set's policies regarding sexual harassment or sexual assault. Additionally, the reported response of the supervisor to earlier alleged complaints must be investigated, as it is likely that if this response is accurate, the company would take disciplinary action. Furthermore, the suggestion that Dawson steals from the company needs to be fully explored in the preliminary interview with Smith to determine whether the suggestions are sufficiently detailed to be included in the preliminary investigative plan. Assuming that adequate detail has been provided, the investigator should make a decision as to whether all three issues (the complaint, the supervisor's response, and the stealing allegation) will be incorporated into one investigation, whether only the claims against Dawson will be included, or whether the claims against Dawson as well as the response of the supervisor will be incorporated into the scope of the investigation. It may be that the claims of stealing are sufficiently vague and broad that a decision is made to conduct an investigation in parallel, anticipating that this will be a far longer and slower process than the more specific claims regarding his alleged inappropriate conduct.

Some helpful questions to explore in determining the proper way to "bundle" issues for investigation (and that can be applied as new issues emerge during the investigation):

- Is the new issue sufficiently related to the existing issue that findings would have an impact on conclusions about the situation as a whole?
- Are the parties central to resolving or exploring the new issue substantially overlapping the existing pool of witnesses?
- If the new issues/allegations are true, would they likely change the organization's course of action relative to the existing organizational scope, or conversely:
  - If the new allegations are found to be untrue, could this substantially affect the assessment of credibility of any party to the current investigation?
  - Is the new issue of sufficient scope that it calls for a separate dedication of resources to ensure that the central investigation is completed in a timely way?

Once the investigator decides, and where appropriate, confirms the scope of the investigation, the best way to execute a disciplined approach is to prepare *investigative questions.*

# Preparing investigative questions

Thinking through all of the questions that an investigation needs answered is an exercise that assists the investigator in maintaining focus and ensures efficiency in execution of the investigation. It provides the investigator an opportunity to take a global view of the complaint and to think broadly about all of the undiscovered, unclear, or disputed areas of the matter. To be very clear, *investigative questions* are separate and distinct from *interview questions*. While interview questions are those things asked of a witness or interviewee, investigative questions are questions an investigator asks of him- or herself. The idea is to consider all of the areas of inquiry necessary to successfully complete the investigation. Investigative questions may include fact inquiries, and questions regarding timing, context, history, relationships, and organizational climate and culture. They may be open-ended (What happened between these parties in the past?) or specific (Did John Doe have access to the cash register during the time in question?).

As an investigative tool, the list of questions should be an actual working document to ensure that an investigator is covering all bases. As some questions are crossed off the list after having been fully explored, new questions may emerge and be added to the list. As an investigator prepares for an interview or considers next steps, this list of questions will remind him or her of areas to explore, resources to tap, individuals to interview, and information to be researched. When all of the items on the list have been fully explored, the investigator can be assured that he or she did a thorough job.

James Wells is a middle manager at Acme Finance company. He recently was considered for but not given a promotion to assistant vice president, a position he alleges he had been promised by Art Gladstone, senior vice president of Acme. Wells has written a letter indicating that he believes the only reason he did not get the position is his Jamaican ancestry. He alleges that this is part of a discriminatory pattern of overlooking non–American born racial minorities.

He points out that the individual who was hired for the position was a less qualified African American.

An investigative plan based on this case might include the following fundamental investigative questions:

- What was the selection process used for this particular promotion?
- What was the selection process used in other promotions?
- What performance management system is being used at Acme?
- Was there any deviation from performance management standards in this situation?
- What is the nature of the relationship between Gladstone and Wells?
- What discussions took place between Gladstone and Wells?
- Who else, if anyone, was party to these discussions?
- With whom did Wells discuss Gladstone's statement(s)?
- What discussions took place between Gladstone and other candidates?
- What role does or did Gladstone play in the selection process?
- Are performance reviews conducted regularly?
- Within the department where Wells works?
- Within other departments?
- Is there a difference in frequency, intensity, or scope between departments or individuals?
- Has Wells had performance reviews?
- What was the nature of those reviews?
- Were they different in frequency, intensity, or scope than others?
- Who received the promotion, and what was this person's experience, background, and performance record like in comparison to Wells?
- Is there evidence of other non–American born racial minorities who have been passed over for promotions?

- What patterns, if any, can be discerned in the promotional practices of Acme within the job category under consideration?

For each of these questions, a path of exploration can then be defined and executed, including review of records, requests for statistical data, interviews with similarly situated employees, and interviews with the principals.

## Policy review

The investigator should, even if he or she is very familiar with an organization's policies, make a careful review of those policies to determine any special or even idiosyncratic language therein to ensure that the nature of policy compliance and violation is clear. Doing so will promote both questions and a line of inquiry, which will allow findings that assist the employer to make a determination as to whether policies have been violated.

In an investigation into possible inappropriate conduct by a public official, an investigator made a determination that a high-ranking official had steered the letting of contracts to her personal friends and associates. Once this was confirmed, the investigator made a report of such to the county executive. The executive pointed out that county policies only considered such behavior misfeasance if the official herself had benefited financially. The investigator had not pursued the investigation sufficiently to make such a determination and had lost the "element of surprise," allowing the official to "cover her tracks" as to whether or not there had been personal gain.

## Ensuring logistical and communications support

The investigator should anticipate logistical requirements and arrange for the dedication of resources that will allow him or her to implement the investigation with the least disruption. The investigator should also be prepared to exercise the "need to know" standard despite organizational pressures that might be brought to bear.

The key decision in this part of planning is to determine how interviewees will be contacted and what they will be told about the investigation. There is some discussion of this in earlier chapters. In general, if the investigator him- or herself cannot make the arrangements, a neutral, nonthreatening individual who does not know the details of the investigation is best to arrange logistics. This is often a confidential administrative assistant in the executive department or elsewhere. It is usually advisable that this person *not* be the same individual who contacts people from a human resources department in routine matters. As discussed earlier, if the investigator is not going to be the one to contact the parties, he or she should prepare a short script for this individual to assist him or her in what to say.

In some matters, there is a need to contact former employees or non-employees, and in other matters the privacy of the parties and the likelihood of reprisal will guide the investigator to contact people at their homes to secure an interview with them. It is best to follow up these requests in writing and carefully document any attempts to contact people outside of the employment setting.

In addition to contacting interviewees, there is a need to let the organization's management know enough to be able to accomplish the investigation. This may simply mean securing release time for witnesses, but it might also involve the implementation of data collection, interim actions to preserve evidence or protect individuals, or ongoing monitoring of communications or conduct. Some officials will need to know there is an investigation, and *some specific information about the nature of the allegations.* Some individuals, particularly those assisting with logistics, will need to know *only that there is an investigation occurring,* without being told the specific allegations. The first group should be tiny or nonexistent, while the second group might be a bit larger.

Although organizational officials are often anxious to know the nature of the allegations or the scope of the investigation, the investigator should be adamant that unless there is a particular reason for the individual to know at the time he or she is making the request, any such disclosures could compromise the investigation and put the person who now knows in harm's way with regard to possible allegations of reprisal and so on.

## Scanning for logistics issues

The investigator should scan for and consider the ramifications of other events in the environment in which the investigation is to be conducted. Specifically, if there are circumstances that could affect the investigation such as a pending reduction in force, vacations, plant closings, acquisitions, schedule changes, management changes, and so forth, the investigator should make recommendations or adjustments to minimize the appearance that any of these actions are related to the investigation or underlying claims.

It is not unusual for organizations to request investigations after "soft interventions" have failed. Sometimes, however, these interventions have not been completed, and continuing with them could be damaging to the investigation.

Morgan Robins has been asked to investigate a series of allegations regarding the conduct of a surgeon at Mountain General Medical Center. In the past month, young female surgical assistants have made four complaints that Dr. Woodson has been behaving erratically, including making uncharacteristically sexual remarks, requesting kisses and hugs, and discussing the shortcomings of marriage. Morgan learns that prior to the time these complaints were made, an organizational consultant was hired to come in and help the surgical team address what was then perceived as "poor conflict management skills." The consultant has signed a contract and is scheduled to arrive in three days to do focus groups and interviews with the team, including the complainants and the respondent.

In this case, Robins has an obligation to ensure that the investigation is being conducted with minimum interference or "static." The confusion likely to be generated by questioning and discussion with entirely different agendas and ground rules would be minimally disruptive; more significantly, it could undermine the integrity of the investigation. Additionally, the assessment process conducted by the consultant could lead to serious problems if complainants believe they are now expected to air their previously private complaints in group settings or if they are placed in focus groups with potential witnesses or respondents. In this particular case, Morgan should urge the employer to delay the beginning of the planned organizational work pending the outcome of the investigation and appropriate remedial action, if necessary. Following the investigation, the organization would need to determine whether there was still a shared belief that the engagement was appropriate and necessary, or whether the scope or nature of the engagement should be altered.

## Customizing notices

As discussed earlier, every individual who participates in an investigation should receive clear and accurate information about the nature of the investigation, the limits on privacy and confidentiality, the process to be followed, and expectations regarding their participation and communications. As part of the preparation for an investigation, the investigator should draft or customize notices to be provided to interviewees. The customization might include specific individuals to be contacted under various situations, instructions about limits on discussion, characterization of the investigation, and identification of the decision-making parties.

## Managing time

Investigations are time- and attention-intensive. They involve deep listening, intense inquiry, critical thought, rapid analysis, and constant reframing of context. While timeliness is important, so is thoroughness and care in conducting the investigation.

The investigator should be sure to generate appropriate expectations for the amount of his or her time and the time of the parties, witnesses, and supportive professionals who may be involved in these investigations. It is unwise, for instance, to schedule back-to-back interviews without proper time for credibility notations, note review, and reflection on what has been learned, not to mention reformulation of questions in light of the most recent information gathered. Time to review relevant documents and time for others to assemble those documents is usually greater than expected.

## Beginning to prepare for interviews

Once the investigator has completed the complainant interview and has generated investigative questions, identifying the persons who will need to be interviewed should be relatively easy. The investigator should consider who will be interviewed and in what order, and should prepare for each interview by identifying key content areas that will need to be explored, and even specific questions that need to be asked. By constructing those questions at the outset, an investigator can ensure neutral, careful wording. On the other hand, an investigator should refrain from limiting interviews in any way based on these questions. Real-time probing and listening will determine the best course of each investigative interview.

# CHAPTER 7

# Special Issues in Interviewing Witnesses

Complainants and respondents generally have a strong interest in being involved in an investigation. Whether it is to get their version of events on the record, to respond to allegations, or to correct or clarify information, there is generally a good deal of motivation to respond to an investigator's request for an interview.

Witnesses are a distinctly different matter. Witnesses are brought into investigations because they may have information that will be helpful to an investigator. Many witnesses, however, would prefer not to be involved in what they may perceive as a "war" between parties. Some witnesses have seen or heard things they would prefer not to explain or discuss, but they do not want to be put in a position in which they must lie to their employer. Still others resent being "dragged into" something they view as none of their business or may have concluded is "a bunch of nothing." This poses two dilemmas for an interviewer: (1) securing the cooperation of uncooperative witnesses, and (2) identifying and finding witnesses who have not been identified by others or have not identified themselves.

# The reluctant or uncooperative witness

Amelia is an employee in the maintenance department. According to her employer, she is well liked, has had perfect attendance, and has been given recognition for good teamwork. Amelia is the only person who can provide eyewitness testimony to an incident that occurred last week.

> It is undisputed that there was a physical altercation between maintenance employees Pat Parker and Roy Melendez in the parking lot outside the main building. Each has presented a different story about what led up to the fight. Although the company has a strict policy against fighting, there is a precedent for relaxing the punishment in cases of clear self-defense. Roy states he was attacked from behind while Pat claims Roy obstructed and verbally provoked him to the point where his pushing Roy out of the way was justified.
>
> Neither individual will concede to any facts alleged by the other. The only thing that both agree on is that Amelia, who was sitting on a bench outside the building waiting to be picked up, heard and saw the entire thing, and she was the one who summoned security when the fight escalated to a brawl.
>
> Amelia is clear that she does not want to speak with the investigator. When she is informed that she must cooperate with the investigation, she goes home ill and misses work for three days, the first time she has ever called in sick.

Dealing with a reluctant witness is a delicate balance of observation, analysis, and excellent listening. In anticipation of conducting the witness interview, an investigator will want to recognize and plan for several steps in dealing with reluctance:

- Identify the organizational imperatives for cooperation, such as policies requiring cooperation, and prepare to be sure that these are communicated early and in a nonthreatening manner.

- Identify any positive feedback provided to the employee by the organization, such as excellent performance reviews, promotions, recognition or awards, and so forth.
- Prepare to determine completely and fully the nature of the witness' relationship with all primary parties in the investigation. This should include researching current and former organizational relationships as well as any known personal or familial relationships, and contacting the primary parties to obtain their description of the relationships.
- Identify the highest priority information that the witness is likely to be able to provide, and prepare to focus on that information should the witness appear likely to terminate the interview.
- Prepare for likely statements of a reluctant witness, such as, "I don't want to get anyone in trouble."

The investigator began the conversation with Amelia by asking questions about her work and history, and noting her accomplishments and successful tenure with the organization. In the course of doing so, the investigator also acknowledged that she was very important to the employer's investigation, and stated that she knew Amelia was aware how important it was to the employer that employees be honest and open with investigators. Aware from prior research that Amelia lived in a nearby community and was a neighbor of Roy Melendez, the investigator acknowledged the challenge of answering questions in such a high-stakes investigation, and gave Amelia a chance to discuss her fears and concerns. When Amelia indicated that she did not see anything, the investigator gently reminded her that both Roy Melendez and Pat Parker had indicated they wanted her to tell the truth. As Amelia became emotional, the investigator focused on the simple question as to whether or not Pat and Roy were facing each other or talking to each other before the fight began, rather than on the fight itself. Finally, as Amelia continued to resist, the investigator stated that the sad reality was that Roy and Pat were both likely to receive discipline or discharge without information that would clarify what happened, and appealed to Amelia's reputation as an honest and forthright person, pointing out that "no one gets in trouble for telling the truth."

The investigator, recognizing that Amelia had up until now evaded direct questioning, changed questioning strategy. Rather than relying on open-ended questions, she posed a set of "yes and no" hypothetical questions, putting Amelia in a position of either lying or telling the truth with no middle ground. As a result, the investigator affirmed Pat Parker's version of events.

**Finding "hidden witnesses":** Sometimes it is simple to find witnesses—events happened within sight or earshot of someone, or an individual has volunteered to one of the parties that he or she has knowledge of an event. Sometimes, however, witnesses are not as readily identifiable, for instance, when events take place outside of the organization's physical boundaries, such as conferences or social events, or behind closed doors when it seems as though there would be no witness testimony available. In these circumstances, the investigator should think through the kinds of testimony that might be *available* and *helpful*.

After closing a significant business deal, Fred and Sam, two attorneys, went out together for a celebratory drink. They remained at the hotel bar for approximately one hour before joining the rest of their colleagues for a dinner with the clients. Later, Sam complained that Fred had made sexual advances while they were at the bar, and that while Sam had clearly rejected the advances, Fred played "cat and mouse" with Sam throughout the dinner. Both agree that there was a significant amount of alcohol consumed during the dinner and that the majority of attendees were intoxicated.

This example represents a common dilemma for investigators attempting to ascertain events while stridently observing the "need to know" standard and also protecting the business interests of parties. The time in the bar involved only the two parties. Those in attendance at the dinner included clients as well as employees, and there is agreement that most would not be able to offer reliable testimony. Given that the parties are attorneys who represent their internal clients, the damage to the party's professionalism could be substantial if the allegations were revealed. In this case, the investigator could struggle mightily to select one or two witnesses most likely to offer helpful testimony, gingerly avoiding questions sufficiently specific to reveal the complaint but specific enough to determine if the witness observed anything amiss. The likelihood that asking "cagey" questions of those in attendance at the party would generate speculation is high.

The best course in this matter, rather than attempting to surgically extract relevant testimony, might be to consider that at any party, and certainly at any bar, regardless of the state of the intoxication of the attendees, there are servers who are omnipresent, presumably sober, and observant. In this case, the investigator could take photographs of Sam and Fred and present them to the bartender or cocktail server, waiters, or bus people at the bar and party, asking if they recalled seeing these individuals and whether they observed or heard conduct or language that made it seem that there was a romantic or sexual interest being expressed. By turning to the servers, the damage to the business deal and relationships is not an issue, and there is far less risk of organizational "leakage" in terms of privacy violations or professional harm.

Similarly, when things occur "behind closed doors," witnesses can often at least verify the whereabouts of the parties, should that be in dispute. Sometimes, it is a witness's observation that someone intentionally followed someone into or out of a room that can tip the scale on credibility.

With witnesses, the investigator must be careful to ask only those questions absolutely necessary; this means that at times, witnesses will be answering questions with little or no contextual framework. It is appropriate to acknowledge that the purpose for the questions might not be apparent, but that the witness is generally better off not knowing more than he or she must know to provide the information being sought.

## Seeking accurate testimony

Workplace investigators must cope with the reality that in general, *the further along the investigation, the less reliable the witness pool.* Despite policies and stern admonitions urging witnesses to refrain from discussing their interview with others in the workplace, some witnesses speak about it anyway, either for strategic reasons or sheer human interest.

Similarly, the primary parties to the investigation are tempted to discuss their respective plights with those they hope will support them. As a result, witnesses are more likely to know of the investigation, to know about specific aspects of the investigation, and perhaps to have "taken sides" as this cascade of information tumbles forward. Therefore, if a complainant identifies someone as a key witness—a person whose testimony could confirm a particular version of facts or who has previously discussed similar behavior with the complainant—it is essential that the investigator make every effort to speak to that witness without allowing the complainant the opportunity to speak with that person. Similarly, when a respondent offers up an individual who can clear him or her or verify his or her version of events, there should be a special effort to interview that witness prior to the respondent's chance to brief this person.

Harry has complained about another employee following him, taking small objects from his office, writing unsolicited cards and notes, and seeking inappropriate proximity to him. He is clearly upset, claiming that the organization has known about this employee's behavior for a long time. He reports that a colleague told him that the former director of human resources received two complaints of similar behavior, but said that although she felt he was dangerous, the organization told her she could not take action because the employee's conduct was not in violation of any policy.

Obtaining a statement from the former HR director would both serve to get a direct statement about any prior complaints, and also assist in establishing if the organization had prior notice of similar conduct. After completing the interview, but before Harry had a reasonable chance of alerting the witness to the subject of the call, the investigator acquired the telephone number for the former head of HR, contacted her, explained her role, and requested a few minutes of her time. In response to a broad question as to whether the HR director had received complaints of conduct she considered to be similar to stalking, she immediately named the employee involved and described taking reports about inappropriate conduct. "I had a bad gut feeling about this guy," she said, "but there was never any proof." Asked if she had expressed a desire to discipline the employee, she denied it. She also refuted discussing the individual with the legal department because "there just wasn't anything there," she said.

## How many witnesses?

Investigators must always strive to interview the smallest number of witnesses possible but enough to ensure that findings are accurate and fully supported. Research on eyewitness testimony suggests that it is not only common but likely that multiple witnesses to the same event will report that differently. Therefore, an investigator will need to consider not only how many confirmatory witnesses (those who agree with a particular version of facts) are to be interviewed, but when witnesses differ on substantive details, how many additional witnesses to seek out.

If 50 people observe an incident, is it necessary to interview all 50? Two? Five? If 30 people in the room report to a person accused of misconduct, and 20 report to the alleged target of the misconduct, does one interview a proportionate number of the respective reports?

Unfortunately, there is no grid or matrix that can answer these questions but an investigator can strive for efficiency. First of all, consider the necessity of interviewing witnesses at all. If there has not yet been a responsive interview, the investigator does not know whether the respondent will deny events or situations. If the complainant identifies a situation and the respondent admits to it, the interview of witnesses will be unnecessary and can seem gratuitous. On the other hand, witnesses can provide clarity and strength to a complaint, or vindicate someone who is accused before they need to be confronted with the allegations.

When identifying witnesses to interview, the investigator should consider the following:

- Do I believe this witness can provide eyewitness or direct testimony regarding an event that is in dispute?
  - If so, have others already provided sufficient testimony to persuade the investigator what happened?
  - Do I have reason to believe this witness's testimony will differ substantively or has the credibility of the other witnesses been problematic?
  - Do I believe this person has information necessary to understand what happened?
- Do I believe this witness actually has information, or am I merely fishing?
  - If it is the latter, is this investigation timely or should I wait to see if the contemplated testimony will be necessary?
  - Was this a witness with whom a complainant or respondent asked me to speak? If so, do I have reason to believe that this individual's

testimony can add to the information I have already gathered?

♦ Is there a witness I can identify who might be less involved or more neutral?

♦ Can I interview this witness without providing essential details of the matter under investigation?

Although these questions may help in decision-making, it is important also to recognize that sometimes one *must* interview many witnesses. Where there is widespread dispute about facts, when there are multiple instances involved in a complaint, or when the potential for clear findings relies on the reliability of witness testimony, the investigator should act in the interest of the accuracy and credibility of the investigation itself. For more on this, see chapter 13.

CHAPTER 8

# Special Issues in
# Interviewing the Respondent

Although it was said earlier, it bears repeating that one of the things an investigator must keep in mind when interviewing a respondent is that in employment investigations, *it is more likely than not that the respondent will continue to be employed by the organization.* An employer, therefore, has every interest in ensuring that the investigation—and each interview—is conducted with an eye toward fairness and treating each individual with dignity and respect. An investigator must to do so while skillfully seeking information in a manner that will get to the truth.

Because an investigator is a neutral party, every effort should be made to follow the same process of interviewing with the respondent as with other parties; developing rapport and creating an environment of trust is extremely important. The investigator should imagine what it might feel like to be brought into an interview knowing that one's livelihood is on the line. The proper demeanor for an investigator dealing with a person accused of wrongdoing is sincerity and openness—sincerity about the fairness of the process, and openness to receive information that may disassemble the investigator's prior thesis about what has happened.

When interviewing respondents, it is best to avoid closed-ended questions until stage four. Although the investigator may believe him- or herself to be thoroughly familiar with the facts, it is appropriate to allow the respondent to "tell his or her story" as completely as anyone else has. Therefore, asking questions such as, "Is it true that you...?" or "Were you at....on this night?" can be counterproductive when the questions should be wide open: "What happened?" or "Can you tell me what you remember about...?" Rushing to the narrow end of the interview "triangle" can actually compromise the fairness and integrity of the investigation, as it does not allow for unknown facts to emerge.

Another reason for delaying a confrontational stage in the interview is the opportunity for the investigator to determine whether the respondent intends to be forthcoming. A respondent who states, "I know why I am here, and I admit what I did, but I'd like to offer an explanation," may be handled in a qualitatively different way by the decision-maker than one who lies, distorts, or resists telling the truth.

Ultimately, every investigator will have to reach the fourth stage of the interview in which the respondent's version of events will be challenged. Here there are several unique interview dynamics to think about: *denials, counterclaims,* and *admissions.*

## Dealing with denials

Denials come in a variety of forms—*simple disputes about facts, claims that the respondent or witnesses are lying, and lack of recollection.*

**Disputes about facts:** In the first case, disputes about facts or context, the proper way to handle the denial is to seek a full explanation from the respondent about what *did* happen.

Jane's subordinate, Kara, has accused Jane of unfair treatment, claiming that while Kara has been disciplined for making personal telephone calls and eating at her workstation, John, her coworker has done both and not been disciplined. Kara has enumerated one specific instance of an extended personal call made by John, and a separate instance of his eating at his station. Jane is asked about the policies and states that she is consistent in enforcing the policies against eating or talking on personal calls. She affirms that she has disciplined Kara and denies that she has failed to discipline John. Jane produces a disciplinary memorandum written to John regarding the extended phone call Kara referred to, pointing out that Kara would have no reason to know whether John was disciplined or not. She reports that John, like Kara, was given a verbal warning in response to eating at his desk on the date in question, pointing out that Kara has received a written warning because she has been caught eating at her station twice.

Making note of the respondent's version of events, soliciting corroboration for the respondent's version, and on occasion, re-interviewing the complainant in light of the respondent's version is the proper course of investigation when dealing with disputed facts.

**Declaring the charges false or malicious:** In some cases, the respondent does not dispute facts or context but declares that the event, situation, or behavior was completely or partially fabricated. This is most common in instances that involve one-on-one behavior where there are no witnesses to support either claim.

Paolo has filed a complaint that his supervisor, Kevin, has been treating him unfairly, and that most recently, when Paolo objected to being omitted from a project team, Kevin became angry and called him a "faggot." Paolo has provided a detailed description of the conversation, describing Kevin's face becoming red and his voice becoming tense. Asked about the conversation that took place, Kevin recalls the conversation becoming "heated." Asked to describe how "heated" it was, he acknowledges that he probably raised his voice and might have used profanity. The investigator inquires into the types of profanity he recalls using, and he states that he does not specifically recall, but that he might have "sworn." When confronted with the allegation that he called Paolo a "faggot," Kevin becomes extremely upset and indicates "that is a completely concocted allegation. I would never, ever use that term here or anywhere else."

There are several ways to respond to a flat denial or accusation that the respondent is lying. One is to ask the respondent to explain why the complainant might have a motive to fabricate, and also to inquire as to whether the respondent has ever had any other experience with the complainant's making false statements. A second, riskier but potentially productive strategy might be to ask a question as a hypothetical, such as, "If I were to inquire of others who have experience with you, would they support your contention that you don't normally make such references?" This question is based on a theory that certain misconduct, such as use of racial or other slurs, is repetitive behavior and can often be established to be a pattern or practice rather than an isolated event. In limited cases, an investigator might want to press the credibility of the respondent by asking, "Would you still deny using the term if I told you others had heard you say the same thing?" Finally, the investigator might challenge the respondent directly: "You admitted that you probably used profanity, but you don't remember what profanity. Is it at all possible that you 'slipped' and said 'faggot'?" These latter strategies are clearly to be saved for the end of the fourth stage of interviewing, as they are highly confrontational and can create an adversarial tone to the interview.

**Forgetting**: "I don't remember" may be one of the most common answers investigators get to their questions. People do forget things, particularly things that don't necessarily register on their personal radar. Thus, witnesses who genuinely wish to be cooperative may actually not remember something because it was not relevant to them at the time it occurred—particularly if the subject they are being asked to recall was not distinctive in any way, such as when someone arrived at work or whether someone went into someone else's office. Claims of forgetfulness become more suspect, however, when unusual or distinctive events and behaviors are part of the query, and even more suspect when those behaviors would have been the respondent's own.

> The bank president recalled the holiday party, the entertainment, and who was there. He remembered leaving the event at approximately 11:30. When asked if he encountered an employee in the parking lot and kissed her, he stated, "I don't remember."

Not remembering incidents that should have been memorable, rather than denying such incidents occurred, should be treated as a likely form of evasion. Follow such a statement of forgetfulness with questions regarding the individual's capacity to remember: Does this person not remember because he or she is or was impaired in some way? Is the conduct so usual and frequent that it was not distinctive? What *does* he or she remember about the incident or event? Ultimately, the investigator should confirm with the respondent that he or she has not denied the conduct, and therefore is stating it is possible that what was alleged did happen. If the respondent agrees with this, it is best to move on and to return to the line of questioning when more context has been attained.

## Counterclaims

Counterclaims can be made by respondents who are denying or admitting conduct. The timing and nature of a counterclaim can inform an investigator about the credibility of a respondent. If, for instance, a respondent is asked about his or her relationship with the complainant, and states that it is positive and professional and full of mutual respect, then later, after hearing the allegations, makes counterclaims to the contrary, this inconsistency should be noted for purposes of assessing the respondent's overall credibility.

Some counterclaims are made to "even the score."

> Harry was accused of telling inappropriate jokes and making sexual comments to his coworker, Janis. When asked about the climate on the work floor, he reported that such behavior was common, and he would engage in such banter himself. Harry is anxious to explain to the investigator, however, that no one has a sense of humor that is smuttier than Janis's, and she is usually the instigator of such behavior. "If I'm going down, then so is she," says Harry to himself.

When receiving such a counterclaim, the investigator should acknowledge the information, thank the respondent for it, and state that it will be useful once the respondent's own conduct has been reviewed. After allowing the respondent to provide his version of the claims under investigation, a second interview structure should be started, with a statement such as, "Earlier in the interview, you made a point that Janis has behaved in conduct that you believe was similar to the conduct you've been accused of. Can you tell me about that?" The interview would then follow the normal, inverted triangle process of any other interview, making the overall structure of this respondent's interview the equivalent of two complete interviews.

Other counterclaims are made to impugn the respondent or to underscore a respondent's motive to fabricate a claim.

> After a request for proposal process, a long-time vendor filed a series of complaints against the director of purchasing, stating that she had manipulated the selection process to deprive his company of several longstanding accounts. Upon being notified of the charges, the director of purchasing stated that she had hoped she would not have to bring the information forward, but that she recently learned that her assistant, who recently left the company,

had a longstanding affair with the vendor and had given his proposals favored treatment. Now that the assistant was no longer there, the director herself oversaw the process and found that the vendor nowhere near met the criterion to keep the accounts.

This type of counterclaim normally warrants a return to the investigative planning process, including an examination of the scope of the investigation. The investigator will need to decide whether to launch a separate investigation or to expand the scope of the current one. Should the counter-allegations, as above, be closely related to the initial allegations, it is likely the investigation would be reframed to take a larger look at purchasing practices involving this vendor. At times, however, counterclaims are unrelated to the initial claim (for instance, someone being investigated for fraud accuses the complainant of sexual harassment), which would call for a separate investigation.

## Admissions

It is the job of an investigator to assist any interviewee in migrating from wanting to tell "their side" to wanting to tell "the truth." This is the logic and theory behind the five stages of interviewing, which allows for the interviewee to be fully heard in a supportive manner prior to being challenged. When an investigator has evidence or witness testimony that is extremely powerful, and a respondent continues to deny, it is appropriate for an investigator to press a respondent for the truth. This might take the form of reminding the respondent of the importance of telling the truth, or it might take the form of revisiting all of the evidence that has mounted counter to the version of events provided by the respondent.

"Robert," says the investigator, "I know you have denied taking the office equipment, but I've got to tell you that I'm struggling with your point of view. Let's go through what

I've already told you. There is a clear electronic record of your entering the office on that Saturday, and only one other person entered that area that day. Do you agree?" Robert nodded his agreement. "You accessed your e-Bay account from the workplace, and when we did so with your stored password, we saw listings for equipment of the same kind for sale under your account."

"I was set up," protests Robert.

"We have two witnesses who say that the day before the equipment disappeared you were upset with your supervisor and told him he was 'going to get what you had coming to you one way or another.'"

"I never said that!"

"Robert, this is just not looking good for you. You cannot explain how the equipment got on to your e-Bay account, you were in the office on the date in question when you had no business reason to be there, and you made statements that appeared to suggest an intention to take something from the company. I need to tell you that it is very much in your interest to tell me the truth at this point, because the next step will be a criminal investigation."

While pressing in this manner will not consistently extract an admission, it can often be persuasive as a respondent sees the heavy weight of the evidence and the inevitable result of the investigation.

Whatever the manner of an admission, the investigator must demonstrate empathy for the respondent. The investigator should thank the respondent for his or her honesty, and acknowledge his or her courage in telling the truth about what happened. It is appropriate to let the respondent know that everything will be done to quickly complete the investigation so his or her future can be more certain.

It is important that the investigator not suggest or imply that telling the truth will result in lesser consequences for the respondent, as this is often not the case. Similarly, the investigator should not in any way suggest what the ultimate determination of the decision-maker might be. Asked "Am I going to lose my job?" the investigator must reply that he or she is not in a position to answer that question, nor would he or she be making the decision as to whether or not the person would be terminated.

Because of the rarity of frank admissions in investigations, an investigator might be inclined to think of an admission as a "win." The investigator should do everything in his or her power to refrain from telegraphing this sentiment in any manner. In fact, it is a sad moment, often a life-changing moment for the person admitting wrongdoing, and it is certainly an unfortunate situation for the company. The solemnity of the admission should be respected and the individual given an opportunity to conclude the interview with respect and dignity.

# CHAPTER 9

# Conducting the Credibility Assessment

Performing a credibility assessment can be the most difficult job an investigator has. The orchestration of an interview may be challenging and exhausting—even maddening—but throughout the course of the interview, and even afterward, the investigator is faced with the even more daunting independent task of assessing the credibility of the party or witness.

Assessing credibility has several phases: an independent assessment of each interviewee's credibility, which takes place during and after every interview, a comparative analysis of credibility as witnesses contradict or dispute one another's version of events, and an independent analysis of the "big picture" as the investigator prepares to make findings.

## Mechanics of credibility assessments

As the investigator conducts and concludes each interview, he or she should note appropriate credibility observations, both objective and subjective, as described below. *These should not be recorded in a manner that would permit them to be mistaken for or intermingled with your interview notes.* Contrary to the thinking of some, it is completely appropriate for an investigator to keep track of his or her impressions, as long as those impressions are clearly distinct from an objective record of what was being said.

In order to maintain the distinction of credibility notations, some investigators simply choose to use a separate color of ink, or preferably, they write their observations on a 3-inch by 5-inch note card labeled with the subject of the interview, the date, and the time. This card can be consulted later in the investigation to remind the investigator of key indicators. Examples of what might be recorded would be significant change in vocal tone or demeanor in response to a particular line of questioning, confirmation of events in opposition to the party's own interest, significant fumbling for words in a witness who was previously fluid and spontaneous in reporting, or statements that are factually dubious and need to be further explored or corroboration sought.

A second tool that is very useful in analyzing credibility, particularly when dealing with multiple perspectives and versions of events, is a simple grid in which each individual's statements are laid side by side with all others, and then reviewed for possible credibility gaps or inconsistency. Categories for such a grid might include "time alleged event occurred," "words used," "identified witnesses," "similar conduct," "response to incident/statement/event," and so on. This is very useful when attempting to determine patterns and consistency of allegations across multiple complaints and different periods of time

Finally, a chronology is an essential tool for conducting a credibility assessment, and allows the investigator to determine whether the time frames described "hang together," or seem logical or credible. Where parties differ as to the timing of events, this can be noted, or alternative times can be listed adjacent to the item in the chronology itself.

January 5th (Complainant) Saw respondent going through his drawers and confronted him by asking him what he was doing in his office. Respondent agrees that he was in complainant's office looking for a file, and indicates that he was picking up file for supervisor because complainant was thought to be out of the office. Supervisor agrees that she requested the file but states that her notes show that this occurred on January 12th (Supervisor), when complainant was out of the office until noon, as confirmed by medical notice from physician. Complainant states that he was not in the office at all on January 12th (vacation request confirms date was asked for, but attendance sheet not completed) and therefore it could not have been on this day. Respondent says he "may" have looked for files in complainant's office more than once but does not recall on which dates.

# Theoretical underpinnings of credibility assessments

**The highly questionable existence of "one truth":** Sit a real estate developer, a Sierra Club member, an engineer, and a daredevil in front of a pristine waterfall and ask them to describe in detail what they see. You will hear earnest, detailed descriptions of entirely different things. Such is the nature of human perception. Some of the differences in perception can be overcome by resorting to a *Dragnet* theory of "just the facts," but even the notion of "facts" becomes a fallacy when dealing with claims of hostile environment harassment; systematic, subtle discrimination; or even habitual patterns of conduct.

A recent investigation involved more than 20 minority witnesses or complainants who had been subjected to discipline for what they considered minor infractions. They were all, in fact, "guilty" of the minor infractions; however, none had heard of any white employees being similarly cited. After careful examination of documents and interviewing a wide variety of employees, the investigator found that when white employees committed similar infractions they were similarly cited; however, it appeared that fewer white employees had engaged in the identical infractions (the investigator ruled out the possibility that supervisors were overlooking the infractions in white employees). The belief that the practices were unequal was widespread, and as a result of the perception of discrimination, many of the complaining employees had become hostile and frustrated, and subsequently were subjected to repeated feedback about diminishing performance, which amplified a sense that they were being targeted and retaliated against (see "the employee issue triad" on p. 152).

This is a typical example of an instance in which employee allegations were brought sincerely and in good faith, based on a legitimate belief they were experiencing discriminatory actions by their employer. Yet the investigation established that the disciplinary actions were consistent across races, despite the appearance to the contrary. Those who demand that the result of investigations reveal "who was telling the truth and who was lying" oversimplify the human experience. To attempt to define "truth" in this situation would defy most conventional versions of the word. The better standard to apply in this and most investigations is a standard by which the investigator examines whether policy violations have or may have occurred, whether perceptions that were reported are reasonable, and whether the employer could have or should have taken steps to address concerns as they were raised. In the matter discussed above, while findings of discrimination were not confirmed, the employer came to an understanding of the context of the complaints and the need for some assistance in improving communication and employee relations in general.

**Telling who is telling the truth:** Part of being a good investigator is simply being a good listener. As discussed earlier, being open, receptive, encouraging, and non-judgmental goes a long way toward getting people to tell their stories. Experienced investigators realize that people have a desire to talk about themselves, to be understood, and to have a listener see the world through their eyes. The good news is that when investigators do their job and interview well, people will disclose things they would hide from others. The bad news is that all people interviewed have a definite point of view, and as such, every event or fact they share may well be distorted by their own history, experience, or emotions.

It is an investigator's job to figure out the objective facts; to siphon off emotion and to identify bias, but to be aware that even within information shared with a particular agenda, there is normally a grain or two of pertinent fact. To complicate matters, truth simply looks different, depending on the speaker.

Sometimes investigators are dealing not with variance in perspective but falsehoods. People lie. They lie for a variety of reasons and in a variety of ways. One study tells us that 48 percent of American workers admitted they had engaged in one or more unethical and/or illegal action during the previous year. Among the most common transgressions were lying to a supervisor or underling, deceiving customers, covering up incidents, taking credit for a colleague's idea, and abusing or lying about sick days. Another study claims that 9 percent of workers admit they tell lies at the office at least once a week, and 15 percent say they've been caught in a lie at work[1].

Given the likelihood that someone may lie during an interview to promote a particular outcome to the investigation, an investigator must be knowledgeable about those things that may be a reliable indicator of untruthfulness. He or she should also know how to approach an individual who may be lying in stage 4 of an interview. Investigators must proceed with caution, however, as the research on spotting lies is not terribly encouraging. There is no expert or machine that can definitively spot a lie. Even the "lie detector," or polygraph,

[1] Rosemary Haefner, Vice President of Human Resources for CareerBuilder.com, in "One in Five Workers Admits to Lying" *HR* magazine, May 1, 2006.

is not foolproof. People who claim to have expertise in this are do no better than those who claim they don't, who in turn do no better than random selection[2].

There is a propensity among many people to subscribe to stereotypes or misperceptions. In a study that asked more than 2,000 people from nearly 60 countries how they could tell if people were lying, the number one answer was the same in every country: They avert their gaze[3]. The problem with this, however, is that it is simply not correlated with lying. Liars don't shift around or touch their faces or clear their throats any more than truth-tellers.

What investigators should note is that there is some behavior that liars are more likely to exhibit than are people telling the truth. Liars tend to move their arms, hands, and fingers less, and blink less than people telling the truth do, and their voices can become higher pitched. People who are embellishing or shading the truth tend to make fewer speech errors, and they rarely backtrack to fill in incorrect details. While all of this is helpful, it is absolutely essential to keep in mind that *just because someone is displaying some or all of these behaviors does not necessarily mean the person is lying.* While researchers point out that they are statistically reliable indicators in groups of research subjects, they are not terribly useful in one-on-one communications.

An investigator's best chance at spotting a liar comes from an analysis of motive combined with observation and circumstance. There are a variety of types of lies, and a variety of types of liars.

Lies can be broken down in lots of ways, but generally, we can lump lies into four broad categories:
1. The pro-social lie, told to help someone else or to protect someone (includes the "white lie").
2. The self-serving lie, which is told to help yourself without hurting someone else ("I got a 99 on the test, Ma.").

[2] Ekman, P., and M. O'Sullivan. 1991. Who can catch a liar? *American Psychologist* 46(September):913–920.
[3] Deception Detection, *Science News* Vol. 166, No. 5, July 31, 2004, p. 72.

3. The selfish lie, which benefits the teller at the expense of another ("Mary never returned my call, so I just did the work myself.").
4. The anti-social lie, which is told to deliberately damage another ("I saw Fred right by the office where the computer disappeared.").

Each of these lies is likely to be used in investigations. Anticipating the purposes of lies, we can often ask questions to ferret out thinking patterns or motives to lie, such as inquiring about perceptions and relationships. If we are faced with a possible pro-social liar, a follow up question might be, "It would be really hard on you if Mary got into trouble, wouldn't it? If that was not the case, might your answer be different?" In other cases, merely seeming skeptical might cause a liar to backtrack and try to change the story.

Given the complexity of making accurate observations about credibility, investigators should observe excellent interviewing practice in order to gauge a person's truthful demeanor, and to spot variance from that demeanor. As advised in the chapter on interviewing, one of the best methods to observe credibility indicators is to "visit" with a subject before diving into the interview. Asking "softball" questions that can be answered without hesitation provides an investigator a clear picture of how the person speaks and responds in an unstressed state. The investigator should make note of the baseline level of tension, the degree of body movement, and the eye contact of a person. This assists the investigator to notice subtle changes and shifts that accompany particular lines of questioning. If an investigator has spotted a clue of possible stress, it is an opportunity to explore consistency and internal logic by asking the same question several ways or asking someone to re-explain something.

The investigator should also watch for some helpful "red flags." Evasion is one of those. Lying to an investigator is a new problem for even a chronic liar. He or she probably knows the investigator is looking for lies and that an investigator may be more skilled than others with whom he or she might normally deal. A witness reporting he or she does not remember something when reason would suggest he or she should, describing only half of the story when it is clear that there is more, or redirecting questions with other questions are all signs the investigator needs to dig further. Another red flag is verbal insulation: Does the person use phrases such as, "At this point in time," "I was led to understand...," or "If I recall correctly..."? These may simply be habitual speech patterns, but careful liars establish "outs" that will let them deny a statement or recollection.

Perhaps the trickiest credibility observation for an investigator is when the investigator's instincts indicate he or she is dealing with an untruth, but he or she is unable to extract an admission or any "hard" indication that this is the case. It is not improper to parse out the reasons for the impression of untruthfulness: Does the person have a clear motive for lying? Did the investigator catch the person lying about other things? Does he or she have a reputation for untruthfulness? Have others stated clearly that he or she "will lie to you"? Has he or she demonstrated contempt for the process, which suggests antipathy toward the complainant or witnesses? If the answer is yes, it is fair to include these as part of an impression that the witness was being less than truthful, but beware of drawing conclusions not supported by those observations.

## Making credibility assessments

Once an investigator has observed baseline conduct, he or she may want to note observations of behavior that is new within the context of the interview and emerges in response to a particular question or line of questioning. This should include the following:

- Startle gestures, such as a sudden eye widening or abrupt movement when faced with a particular question.
- Broken eye contact
- Unnatural or inconsistent hesitancies

- Flushing or coloring
- Change in pitch of voice

Investigators should also note observations of *conduct contrary to self-description* (e.g., the highly confrontational witness who states he or she is "timid.") Although these may be thoroughly documented, the investigator should never draw conclusions about these observations in their credibility notations or in isolation.

Certain observations should be made with care. For instance, disassociation is common among those describing troubling experiences, resulting in some extremely traumatic incidents being described in a bland or matter-of-fact manner. Investigators should not assume that minimal effect equals minimal impact. Similarly, investigators should not over-interpret a highly calm response to serious allegations. It is a simplistic notion that innocent people are all furious at being falsely accused of something. This is an area where cultural and subcultural differences, socio-economic differences, and workplace culture can influence demeanor, and investigators should be extremely careful of observations made in this regard.

Things that are legitimately attributed to credibility, and which should be well documented, include subtle or direct attempts to influence the outcome of the investigation through inducement or threat, or statements or nonverbal clues that suggest cognitive dissonance or skewed view of reality.

> While being interviewed regarding allegations that as the only woman in the accounting department she was treated poorly, the complainant listed a number of situations and circumstances to support her claim. During the uninterrupted initial narrative, she became quite upset and said, "And then there are those horrible magazines," as she broke down sobbing. "Magazines?" prompted the investigator, "Yes—those filthy, horrible magazines. *Glamour, Redbook,* and *Modern Bride.* Someone leaves them in the break room once a month, and they are filthy, full of [in a mock whisper] S-E-X."

In this matter, the apparent thin-skinnedness of the complainant was noted, and this particular exchange highlighted by the investigator as a possible indication of unreasonable propensity to see things as offensive or sexual.

## Interviewer feedback

In a case where, for instance, an individual has been said to be behaving in a manner that is intrusive or offensive, and the interviewer makes observations of such behavior (i.e., pulling chair into close proximity to interviewer, touching him- or herself in a suggestive manner), it is appropriate to inquire in a reasonable way as to whether such behavior is intentional, or if the subject of the interview is unaware of such behavior.

> An individual who was accused of gazing inappropriately at women's breasts was observed by the investigator to be casting his eyes toward her chest in a consistent manner during the interview. "I know you have insisted you have not looked at women inappropriately, but what I am observing now is that you are looking toward me in a manner consistent with what others have described happening to them. Can you tell me what you are looking at, or where you believe your eyes are focused?"

## Corroboration

In the "he said, she said" world of employment investigations, it is a rarity, albeit a pleasing rarity, to find a "smoking gun," such as physical or photographic evidence that makes a particular version of events indisputable. Yet there are many sources and strengths of corroboration that investigators should consider.

Corroboration is either material or incidental verification of a report by an independent source.

**Strong corroboration**: This includes physical evidence or multiple, impartial, or uninvolved witnesses providing similar observations or experiences, such as eyewitnesses, surveillance tapes, e-mails, or spreadsheets supporting fully one version of events.

**Simple corroboration**: This includes contemporaneous reports to neutral or uninvolved individuals, contemporaneous documentation transmitted to an organizational representative or other credible third party, or a single impartial or uninvolved witness providing similar observations or experiences. Conversations with managers about concerns, letters written to compliance organizations, even reports to therapists that coincide with the timing and nature of events as they were reported give credence to a particular version of events.

**"Rule out" corroboration**: This is actual evidence supporting two differing versions of the same event (e.g., receipts from two different restaurants from the same night and time) or conclusively ruling out the possibility that something transpired as it was described.

A witness alleged to have engaged in after hours misconduct in the office on a particular evening produced a passport and travel documents proving that he was not in the country on the date the event occurred.

# History and patterns of behavior

Past conduct is generally but not always an indicator of future conduct. A history of similar events adds credibility to an alleged current event. A history of false complaints compromises the credibility of a current complainer. A history of untruthfulness should be considered when evaluating the likelihood of current truthfulness. Additionally, asking the following questions can be helpful:

- Aside from the time of the incidents, was the conduct of the parties consistent with their description of the overall environment (e.g., employee complains of hostile work environment but often remained in the work area long after shift ended)?
- Do others report an alleged bad actor behaving in a similar but not as egregious manner toward them?

■ Are there witnesses who consider themselves to be "supporting" the accused but still verify conduct (while interpreting intent differently)?

## Indeterminate credibility

Although investigators have reasonable latitude to make choices as to whether or not their impressions and observations are sufficiently clear to lead to credibility assessments, so too can they conclude that credibility determinations cannot be made. There simply are times where the interaction between interviewee and interviewer is not conducive to such observations, as well as situations in which all parties have similar motives to be honest or to lie. In some cases, an investigator might find all of the witnesses unbelievable or all of them equally credible. *Saying so is not a failure on the part of the investigator or an investigation.* Rather, it is consistent with the duty of an investigator to make findings based on the weight of the evidence, rather than forcing equally balanced evidence to bias one way or another.

## Credibility assessments in a written report

There are a number of ways a credibility assessment can be drafted. Several examples can be found in appendix C.

# CHAPTER 10

# Gathering Evidence

One of the most significant aids in finding facts is the examination of evidence. Physical or electronic evidence can be an investigator's best friend when there are disputed versions of facts or varying descriptions of events.

There are many sources of evidence. This chapter will consider the most common, but investigators must be creative and resourceful in thinking through all of the opportunities to find scraps of physical, electronic, or other evidence that might tip the fact-finding scales in a particular direction.

## Internal documents and records

Personnel files, attendance records, performance reviews, memoranda, background checks, insurance forms, cell phone bills, telephone records, court filings, and other internal documents are a primary source of evidence. These documents can reveal new information or support information that had been provided to the investigator. Since these records are readily available to the investigator, their review should be a routine part of any investigation. It is important to remember that while an investigator may not feel a need to examine a personnel file, it may well be a source of previously undiscovered information.

Sam Jones had been a subject of discussion by many witnesses. Many stated he was a violent and abusive manager who was widely known for his cruel treatment of employees. Although witnesses described individual incidents, they were always one-on-one confrontations, away from any witnesses or surveillance equipment. Sam and his supervisory colleagues insisted that incidents and general descriptions of Sam's conduct were fabrications of disgruntled employees. A review of Sam's personnel file seemed to shed no light on the disputed characterization of his demeanor until the investigator noted an entry from five years prior regarding a mandatory Employee Assistance Program referral. The EAP provider was no longer under contract by the employer, and the manager making the referral was no longer employed by the organization, but through a careful search, the investigator found and secured an interview with the referring manager.

After persuading the manager that she was not bound by any confidentiality with regards to actions she took while employed by the organization, she reluctantly described an "awkward situation," which involved Sam becoming "somewhat obsessed" with a coworker, and managers scrambling to determine what should be done. "We didn't have any policies that covered it, and the employee begged us to keep it confidential," she explained. Subsequently, the investigator was able to determine that an employee had made a complaint of stalking involving Sam, and that Sam had admitted the conduct and been sent to EAP and ordered to have no contact with that employee. When asked why he had not disclosed that in light of the investigator's questioning, Sam stated that he had "forgotten the whole thing." This evidence was helpful to the investigator in evaluating Sam's credibility and adding credence to a pattern of inappropriate workplace conduct.

Many investigators submit a written request to preserve documents to ensure they are not destroyed or altered during the course of the investigation. A copy of such a letter is attached as appendix D.

**Witness-generated documents and electronic records:**
In chapter 7, one of the "core" interviewing questions involving inquiries as to whether the interviewee had, him- or herself, generated any documents pertinent to the issues or events discussed in an interview. These documents might include notes intended to serve as contemporaneous documentation, calendar entries, diaries or journals, correspondence (letters, e-mails, and memoranda), voicemail recordings, e-mails sent or received, telephone messages, to-do lists, or other documents unique to the situation.

Once an interviewee has identified the existence of a witness-generated document, it is in the interest of the investigator to acquire that document as soon as is practical. The reality is that once a document is revealed, and prior to the time that document is in the possession of the investigator, the investigator cannot prevent the document from being altered or even invented for purposes of supporting the interviewee's version of events. Therefore, an investigator should be aggressive in his or her efforts to acquire documents as soon as practicable.

During the preliminary interview with complainant Michael Thomas, he provided a detailed list of events pertinent to his complaint. Asked if he made any notes while these events transpired, Michael told the investigator that he keeps a daily journal, and that each of these events had been noted contemporaneously in that journal. The investigator, anxious to acquire the relevant journal entries, asked Michael if he had brought the journal with him.

He responded that he had not, as there were other journal entries that were private, and he was unwilling to turn the journal over to the investigator in its entirety.

The investigator suggested that Michael could select the pages the investigator would review or copy, or that, preferably, the entire journal could be copied with the irrelevant material eradicated. Michael agreed to the former and offered to deliver the relevant pages to the investigator.

The investigator suggested it would be important to see that the pages were part of a larger journal, and asked that Michael bring the book itself to him.

Michael agreed, and the investigator offered Michael a break to retrieve the journal from his home. Michael stated that he had no way to return home and back in a timely manner, as the public transportation availability was intermittent during the middle of the day. The investigator offered Michael cab fare to go home and retrieve the journal, or to drive Michael to his home to retrieve it, and Michael stated he was not exactly sure where the journal was, and would bring it in the following day.

When the journal was turned in and the relevant pages copied, the investigator was suspicious about Michael's hesitancy to produce the document immediately, and retained a handwriting expert to examine the document. The expert determined that there was an extremely high probability that the journal entries, although dated months and weeks apart, had been written in a single sitting.

**Third-party documents and records:** Depending on the nature of the matter under investigation, there may be documents or records available from third parties that would be helpful to investigators. In some cases, acquiring these records will require the consent of the parties involved, and in other cases they can be acquired with the help of others. These include the following:

- Medical or therapeutic records
- Driving and licensing records
- Charge account records
- Banking records
- Surveillance tapes or photographs (such as those taken at ATMs or compliance recordings of telephone transactions)
- Data card records
- Photographs taken for publicity or other purposes
- Third-party correspondence (such as applications or enrollment records)

- Attendance records for external events
- Broadcast recording
- Travel documents

In most cases, the easiest way to obtain these records is with the consent and the cooperation of the subject.

Investigators should draft or obtain a simple release form that can be signed, dated, and customized to allow the investigator to examine documents and to describe the handling and retention of those documents for the purpose of the investigation. In cases where the investigator wishes to acquire these documents surreptitiously, there may be substantial legal obstacles to doing so. Although in the case of credit records or driving records, an employee may have already provided consent for the employer to gain access to those records, and such consent can be used by the investigator to acquire those records, other records, such as telephone and banking records are much more difficult to acquire, and investigators should work with counsel to determine appropriate means of requesting those records. It is ill-advised to impersonate others or to misrepresent one's role in order to acquire those documents that would not normally be available to the employer.

**Creative evidence collection:** Apart from documents and electronic records, there are often other pieces of evidence that could be of value to an investigator. These might include receipts or purchase records of retailers, mementos retained by a party (such as matchbooks or menus), sign-in sheets at events or exhibits, photographs, even items of clothing (such as the infamous "blue dress" belonging to Monica Lewinsky). Investigators should be courageous about seeking such evidence, recognizing that there is nothing wrong with asking for items or records as long as one is not lying about the purpose of asking.

The assistant vice president of human resources has been accused of engaging in numerous inappropriate relationships within the organization. Several women have reported being "courted" by him and others have reported receiving unwanted gifts and flowers. Although they have produced everything from lingerie to flowers, all report that these gifts have arrived without any card and that they were followed by a phone call from the AVP announcing that the items were gifts from him.

The flowers had all been sent from different floral shops, but the investigator has approximate dates for each. There is no record of these purchases on the AVP's corporate credit card. The investigator requests that the CEO's administrative assistant call each floral shop and identify herself, and that she state she is attempting to verify a purchase by the AVP on or approximately on the date in question. Although two of the floral shops state that they cannot provide purchase information, four others readily verify the AVP made the purchases and paid by his personal credit card. The investigator then requests that AVP provide a release in order for the investigator to acquire a record of charges to specific vendors. When faced with this request, he admits purchasing and sending flowers, offering a new explanation for the earlier denials.

In addition to actually gathering physical and electronic evidence, it is appropriate to take digital photographs of physical settings, locations, and items that are important to memorialize or will be helpful to those attempting to reconstruct the steps taken by the investigator.

**Collecting and cataloguing evidence:** Whenever possible, the investigator should inspect original records, rather than accepting photocopies. Photocopies should be made while the interviewee who has provided them is still present, and the investigator may choose to have the interviewee initial each copy to attest to its accuracy. In cases of large amounts of documents, the investigator may provide a form filled in at the time the documents are retained for photocopying that indicates the nature and quantity of documents collected, that the photocopies were inspected and are accurate, and that originals were retained or returned. Similarly, if objects are provided to the investigator, the investigator should create a digital photograph and obtain a signed form from the subject that indicates the objects, that the photograph is an accurate representation, and that the object was returned.

It is critical that evidence retained in the file be maintained in an organized manner, most often catalogued by the provider of the information. The use of Bates numbering systems is an option but not required.

## Physical electronic evidence: using experts

Forensic experts can assist in uncovering hidden information on computers, in documents and files, and in e-mail systems. In-house IT people can usually assist in retrieving instant messages and Internet use patterns, as well as sites visited. Some employment investigators and attorneys have developed specialized knowledge in this area, but it is also perfectly acceptable to view this as an area for consultation with experts. Expert handwriting analysis, even chemical lab analysis of substances alleged to be illicit drugs, can be part of the routine collection and analysis of evidence in employment investigations. Be sure when using experts to have an unassailable chain of custody of the evidence and to include the expert report in the investigative file.

## Maintaining chain of custody

In most cases, investigators will collect and retain documents, or copies of those documents, and the documents will not leave the possession of the investigator. If at any time there is a need to submit evidence for examination by a third party, the investigator should document the chain of evidence by noting when the document was given to the third party, and having the third party sign a notice attesting that the evidence remained under his or her supervision prior to its return to the investigator. The return time should be noted as well.

# CHAPTER 11

# Taking Notes

There is no one right way to take notes. But the hallmark of a good note-taker is that he or she can reconstruct what was said with a high degree of accuracy, even after the passage of time. For some, this is accomplished with a pen and legal pad and an elaborate system of abbreviations and shorthand. For others, it is accomplished with highly developed keyboarding skills and a laptop computer. Every investigator will find a method he or she is most comfortable with, and then improve the accuracy and efficiency of his or her note-taking in only one way—by taking notes as often as practical until the practice is second nature. Taking notes should be as unobtrusive as possible during an interview, particularly during the earliest stages of an investigation.

Investigative notes should be even-handed, neutral, and complete. To the extent possible they should reflect the actual words used by an interviewee, rather than the investigator's characterization of those words. Notes should always include the question to which an interviewee is responding and questions that an interviewee could not or did not answer. These notes need not be detailed, or even understandable to anyone other than the investigator, but to the extent the investigator does understand them, that understanding should be enduring, as the "gold standard" for investigative notes is that an *investigator should be able to rely on his or her notes to reconstruct each interview months or years after the interview took place.* Based on the need for durability, an investigator should consider taking steps to ensure the quality of his or her notes.

As a matter of practice, notes should be reviewed as part of the final stage of any interview, with the investigator reviewing what has been said, making any clarifications, and closing any gaps that are apparent on review. In essence, by recapping the interview with the interview subject, the investigator is confirming the accuracy of his or her notes. Following the interview, the interviewer may choose to sit down with the notes and to improve their clarity by eliminating potentially confusing abbreviations, correcting spelling or grammar to better reflect what was said, or adding detail too extensive to be captured at the time of the note-taking but fresh in his or her memory. If the notes were handwritten, the investigator may wish to transcribe them. There is nothing improper about doing this *as long as the additions, corrections, alterations, or clarifications are distinct and clear from the actual notes.*

In the case of notes taken on a laptop, this is easily accomplished by saving the original version of the notes and then making a second document with additions. It is helpful to make those additions in a colored ink or separate font so they can be easily identified without a need to electronically compare versions. For those using handwritten notes, enhancements can be made on a separate sheet of paper, in a distinctly different colored ink, or on a photocopy of the original notes. The original notes should always be retained, in addition to any "clean up" or "clarification" documents.

Notes, of course, should reflect only what has been asked and said. There is some latitude to note pertinent actions or events of the witness (for instance, it is appropriate to note when breaks were taken or when a witness begins to cry), but these observations should be brief and parenthetical. Good notes will allow a "read back" of the conversation, including conditional statements and deflective comments or asides, to ensure that an investigator is working from the best record possible.

Some organizations have witnesses sign the investigator's notes. The thinking behind this is that it ensures that a witness agrees with what was said. The problem, however, arises if an interviewee regrets having made an admission or disclosure and states at the time of signing that he or she did not, in fact say what the notes reflect. This places the investigator in a curious dilemma. Is the investigator to now delete what he or she heard? Does the retraction or denial of the witness render the overall interview invalid? Is the witness's signature necessary to attest to the accuracy of the interviewer's notes? To avoid these sticky questions, it is best to allow notes to serve their purpose—both as a record for the investigator and to implement the use of separate signed statements if an employer wishes to have a witness-generated document of any type.

# CHAPTER 12

# Generating an Investigative Report

Reporting the results of the investigation can take several different procedural paths; in cases where litigation is anticipated, attorneys will often request a verbal report first, and then make a decision about whether they wish to receive a written report. The verbal report should be made by creating an outline based on the format for the written report. Although the investigator's notes will be in writing, they will lack the detail of the ultimate written report and should contain only that information necessary for the investigator to report thoroughly and accurately.

In routine investigations, most policies and procedures call for a written report. This report should be first assembled as a draft and submitted to the decision-maker for review. The reason for this is that frequently those making the decisions request more information, point out additional witnesses they think might be helpful, or find that the report itself needs clarification. For this reason, most investigative reports are rewritten, at least in part.

Unlike notes, in which the original version is most critical, drafts of reports should be destroyed when the final version is complete. By virtue of being a draft, and not a final product, the investigator is acknowledging that it is an imperfect or incomplete document, and therefore it should not be part of the permanent record.

A written investigative report should be formatted in a manner that is useful for the reader and provides sufficient information to support any conclusions. Although there can and should be some variance in formatting, depending on the complexity of the investigation, overall content of a report should be consistent.

# Part 1 – the rationale for the investigation

The first part of a report should explain why the investigation was begun. If it was in response to a complaint, the date of the complaint and the process of deciding to investigate should be included. If the writer is an outside investigator, the section should include the date of retention and the information provided at the outset of the investigation, as well as the source for that information.

This investigation was conducted in response to a written complaint submitted to Mary Smith on April 12, 2001, containing several allegations regarding the record keeping in the law department. Ms. Smith met with the complainant on April 13 and determined that a neutral investigation was necessary.

# Part 2 – the methodology for the investigation

This section can be customized from the boilerplate developed by each investigator, as investigative methodology will be consistent from one case to another. Minimally, this section should include any decision-making about how the investigation was conducted; location and conditions of interviews; notices provided to those providing information; documents or other evidence obtained by the investigator; how notes were taken and kept; and any unusual or exceptional conditions under which the investigation took place, as well as any restrictions that were imposed on the investigator or the investigation.

In order to conduct this investigation, I interviewed 11 individuals. In addition to the complainant, this included individuals who were the subject of the complaint, those alleged to have received complaints from the complainant, those who were alleged to be the target of inappropriate conduct, as well as those who could verify or refute certain facts.

In addition, I examined communications between and among the complainant and respondent, and other employees, as well as the e-mail inboxes of certain individuals. Certain communications were provided to me by interviewees, and all were authenticated, examined, and incorporated into the findings in this investigation.

In each interview, I began by explaining my role. Specifically, I informed each interviewee that Large Law Firm had retained me to conduct an investigation into alleged misconduct. I specifically explained that I was neither an attorney nor an advocate of any kind, but rather that I was a neutral fact-finder with no predisposition as to the outcome of the investigation.

Each interviewee was informed that I would be taking notes, that those notes would remain in my possession, and that I would be making a report to Large Law Firm. They were instructed that they were expected to cooperate with the investigation but urged to ask any questions or seek any advice necessary to ensure that their participation was accurate and voluntary. They were each advised that information would be shared only if it were necessary to conduct a thorough investigation. Further, interviewees were advised to minimize unnecessary discussion of this investigation with others in order to assist the investigator. All interviewees were informed that if the investigation revealed a violation of employer policies, those individuals who violated the policies could be subject to discipline up to and including discharge. Finally, each was informed that reprisal or retaliation against anyone who participated in the investigation would be responded to promptly and remedially. Each interviewee was given the opportunity to ask questions at the outset and at the conclusion of the interview, and each interviewee was given my business card and invited to contact me directly if they wished to impart additional information after the conclusion of the interview.

# Part 3 — summary of allegations

This is essentially a capsule of the interviews with the complainant(s) and any additional allegations that emerged over the course of the investigation. It is extremely helpful to a reader if these can be listed item by item in outline or numbered form.

1. Complainant alleges that she was ordered by her direct supervisor, Stanley Jones, to enter false data on the weekly financial reconciliation report. This occurred on January 15 at 3 P.M., and was in reference to the report for January 1–7.
    A. Specifically, complainant states that Jones instructed her to deduct $300 from the "entertainment" line item and to add $300 to the "general office" line item.
    B. Complainant states that she was working from actual expenditure data and knew this entry would not be accurate, so she asked Jones why he wanted to "fudge" the data.
    C. Complainant states that Jones became angry and told her "just do your job or find a new one." She states that she refused to enter the data and was told by Jones she had better start looking for a new job.
    D. Complainant states that she immediately contacted human resources and made the complaint that resulted in this investigation.
    E. Complainant states that this is the first and only incident in which she is aware that Jones has asked her to enter false data.

# Part 4 – summary of witness statements

This section should include a summary of each witness' statement and be directly responsive to the items in part 3, so witness testimony can be reviewed as it applies to each allegation. In general, it is a good idea to avoid putting witnesses' names in reports, instead identifying them as "witness A" or "witness 1." The rationale for this is that the decision-maker who will read the report does not need to know who the witnesses are, so their identities do not belong in the report. Exceptions should be made in two cases:

1. When the witness is a manager or supervisor, and therefore what he or she saw, heard, or experienced served as notice to the organization.
2. When the identity of the witness is essential to understanding why credibility was deemed high or low.

# Part 5 – statements respondent(s)

The statement of the respondent should be completely responsive to every allegation in part 3, as well as including any new information or contextual clarification provided by a respondent.

Smith denies ever telling complainant that she was beautiful or making comments about her skin color. He does acknowledge that he may have said he was glad to see her or that seeing her " brightened his day" on the date in question, since she had been on vacation the prior week. Smith states that he would make a similar comment to any other member of the support staff. Smith states that he tends to compliment people, and has probably complimented complainant on her attire, which tends to be "exotic." Asked what "exotic" meant, he stated, "Ethnic. Brightly colored." Asked if he specifically told complainant that he found her attire "exotic," Smith reported that he did not recall, but admits that he "might have." Smith acknowledges that he may have on occasion told complainant or others that he found them "delightful," but specifically denies targeting or focusing on complainant or making personal statements about her attractiveness or ethnicity.

# Part 6 — discussion and analysis of evidence

In this section, any evidence the investigator reviewed should be listed, and relevant analysis discussed. This should also describe any physical inspections the investigator has done, such as visiting a location to determine its layout or bringing a witness to a location to identify specific aspects of the event witnessed.

The investigator inspected payroll data and HRIS records for the past 24 months for evidence of age or gender discrimination as alleged.

1. An analysis of workforce composition and monetary compensation showed that the average age of Acme employees is 37, and that the average salary of the employees earning more than $50,000 (n = 45) is $98,183. The class of employees being compensated above $50,000 annually will be referred to as high comp (HC) in this report.

2. The average salary for HC males is $86,552 and for the HC females $71,712. This should be examined in light of the gender composition of the twelve executive (most highly compensated) positions, which are composed of 10 males and three females.

3. Of the 12 HC employees in the executive group, 10 were born prior to 1966 (40 years old by 12-31-05) and 2 were born later than 1966.

4. Sixteen people in the HC group were involuntarily terminated during the past 24 months because of restructuring or performance issues. Eight of these were born prior to 1966. Eight were born afterwards. Fourteen were male and two were female.

The investigator reviewed the complainant's personnel file and found two memoranda dated 12/12/99 and 12/30/99, each stating that the complainant had arrived late after being warned. Both memoranda were from Mike

Jones to the complainant. The first memorandum states that the employee was 14 minutes late on that date and that a second occurrence of lateness will result in discipline, and the second states that the complainant was being placed on six months of disciplinary probation due to arrival six minutes late on that date. Copies of these memoranda are attached as Appendix A and B.

No conclusions should be made or inferences drawn in this section. The investigator will need to make a distinction between information that can be presented in cumulative or analyzed form (the first example) or a need to present evidence as part of the report itself (the second example.) To the extent that findings will depend on specific evidence, it is best to make the evidence available to the reader in some form. Digital images of physical evidence or reproduction of key documents are appropriate as appendices.

## Part 7 – credibility assessment

There should always be a section discussing credibility in an investigative report, even if the entire section is a statement that the investigator was unable to make credibility determinations. As discussed in chapter 9, there are many forms that credibility assessments might take— from a brief discussion of investigator observations to detailed analysis of corroborative testimony.

Jane Jenkins's testimony was deemed to be highly credible, as she acknowledged the event with full awareness that doing so could result in her own termination. Jane's demeanor was consistent with an individual troubled by "keeping a secret," and her emotional testimony was detailed and specific.

Roberts stated that he refused to answer his cell phone because his caller ID showed that it was Bates who was calling. Asked to scroll back through his caller ID memory on his cell phone, Roberts was able to see caller ID from all calls dating back 10 days to April 1, 2006. Bates's name and number was not included in those viewable by scrolling through all received calls. Roberts's claim that Bates had called him on April 3, 2006, was determined to lack credibility. Upon further investigation, the investigator established that Bates's home and cell numbers are "blocked" and would not have been visible on a caller ID. Roberts's credibility overall is diminished by this clear untruth.

# Part 8 — findings

The final part of a report is the findings of fact. These findings should be streamlined but sufficiently detailed to allow a reader to understand precisely what transpired. Although at times it is possible to make a finding that a report was "substantiated," "unsubstantiated," or "indeterminate," if the complaint involves more than a single incident, or if new allegations or counterclaims have surfaced during the investigation, there will need to be several sections to your findings. Therefore, findings may simply be a recitation of "what happened," rather than determinations about the validity of claims.

Complainant has alleged that she was subjected to harassment by respondent on several occasions:

1. On January 5, 2006, complainant and respondent were in Omaha, Nebraska, attending a company training program.

A. Respondent placed 14 calls to complainant's room using the hotel telephone system between the hours of 7 A.M. and 8 A.M.

B. Some time before 9 A.M., the respondent was observed standing in the hotel corridor and speaking in a loud voice while facing the door to the complainant's room.

C. At 8:55 A.M., the complainant telephoned the hotel security office and stated that she was "scared my coworker has gone crazy," and she was "terrified to leave her room" because the coworker was "stalking her."

D. At 9:00 A.M., the respondent appeared at the scheduled training class and indicated that he had tried to find the complainant but she did not answer her door or telephone, and stated to the class that she "probably had a rough night."

E. At 9:05 A.M., complainant reported to Hal French, hotel security chief, that she had been threatened and harassed by respondent by telephone and by his repeatedly knocking on her door and demanding that she speak to him.

Note that in the above example, no conclusions are reached as to the propriety of the events or whether they might constitute harassment. Enumeration of these events would be followed by a more conclusive statement.

Based on the events above, respondent engaged in a pattern of behavior that had the effect of interfering with the complainant's ability to perform her job functions and reasonably caused her fear in her personal and business life.

It is critical that every word of the findings being made is supported by everything that has preceded it in the report. After drafting findings, it is helpful to review the sections of the report that support a particular finding and to create a "working index" should there be questions regarding the reasoning or analysis that led to particular findings.

CHAPTER 13

# Conducting Investigations Into Systemic Issues and Hostile Environment

Increasingly, organizations are being confronted with claims that do not involve allegations limited to specific incidents but that the organization (or parts of the organization) is permeated with hostility toward a particular protected class. Investigating such allegations is somewhat different from looking into specific complaints because the investigator is attempting to discern cultural norms, broad-based assumptions and patterns, and practices over time. Unlike an investigation involving a small group of people who are alleged to have either been involved or been witness to particular conduct, each person in the organization is a witness to the functioning of that organization, and each likely has a unique perspective about that organization.

In a large urban medical center, employees in the respiratory medicine clinic had the highest rate of turnover. There had been five separate investigations over the past three years in response to complaints of discrimination, harassment, and patient care irregularities. None of these investigations turned up any actionable information, despite

115

findings that there were relationship issues and fear of certain managers. When a sixth complaint was filed, the center administrator decided that responding to individual complaints was preventing leaders from seeing the "big picture," and they assembled a team to conduct an overall investigation into the working environment in the respiratory medicine clinic. With more than a hundred staff members, 30 physicians (some not employees), and 50 nurses, the investigation would need to be well designed.

# The importance of planning

The investigative plan (see chapter 6) is important in any investigation, but when taking on the investigation of climate and culture, planning becomes the linchpin of an effective investigation. In particular, the investigative questions should be carefully thought through to serve as a compass to ensure appropriate focus and depth of the investigation. If a fact-based investigation *can* go astray, then a systemic investigation is *likely* to go off course without the discipline of monitoring scope and strategy constantly.

Beginning with what is known, the investigator should establish a list of content areas to be explored and a set of questions within each content area. As more concerns or issues are raised, they can be added to the matrix of issues. As the matrix expands, the pool of potential interviewees will naturally expand, as will the nature of the questions to be asked to interviewees. By planning appropriately, both interview questions and the sampling of interviewees can be accomplished in an efficient manner.

Sample questions for an investigative plan for an urban medical center respiratory medicine clinic are listed in the table on the following page.

After a set of investigative questions has been laid out, the next step is to plan the interviewing and evidence-gathering necessary to explore the questions.

It is particularly important to seek a *broad sampling* of interviewees when investigating overall work environment. Also be sure that the sample selected includes a valid

| Area of Concern | Alleged Targets | Questions |
|---|---|---|
| Pay/comp-ensation | Women, Latinos | Are there inequities in starting salary, bonus, raises, or salary/tenure ratios? Scale? Size? Methods of calculation? Administration? |
| Scheduling | Women | Are all policies regarding overtime being complied with? Have all employees had equal access to opportunities to expand their hours? How have scheduling procedures been communicated to employees? Have there been different communications? |
| Training and development | Latinos, African Americans, other racial and ethnic minorities | How have training and development opportunities been allocated? Have there been denials of training opportunities? If so, who and why? Are there inequities in approval/disapprovals by supervisors? What is the racial composition of training classes? Any patterns? |
| Physician relationships | Physicians | What conflicts exist between physicians? To what extent have those conflicts been discussed in the work environment? What has been communicated to staff and nurses regarding conflicts? Specific issues among longer tenured doctors? How have conflicts affected patient care? Have staff members been asked to take sides? Are physicians interfering with one another's work? |

representation of those groups or individuals alleged to be targeted. In fact-finding investigations, the investigator is operating in a narrow scope and attempting to limit the witness pool to only those who are likely to have specific information. In these systemic matters, an investigator spends less time attempting to confirm or clarify specific events and more time acquiring a full and diversified perspective of what happens within the work environment. The investigator is interested in everything from communication to leadership conduct, to events and responses to events. When seeking out people to speak with in a systemic investigation, any witness could transform into a complainant or respondent. Thus, in addition to speaking to those with known grievances, the investigator will need to select others to generate an appropriate sample.

In environmental investigations in large organizations, it is best to methodically sample the population when selecting individuals to interview. This can be done by using employee lists and selecting a particular interval—for instance, every third or fifth employee on the alpha list, and asking those employees to participate in interviews. It can also be done by creating a matrix of factors such as tenure, job family, and protected class status, and randomly selecting from those subpopulations. The anticipated result is that the interviews will vary considerably from one another.

In some cases the investigator will find that interviewees have little to say, while some will not only have a great deal to say but will suggest others who should be interviewed. When receiving an interview "referral" of this type, investigators should inquire as to the nature of the information that the referring witness believes that the person could provide, and to consider the questions recommended in chapter 7 to determine whether the referral should be accepted. It is also important to recognize that while those people who are unhappy in an organization will generally encourage the investigator to speak to others with similar perspectives, the same may not be true for those who are content. Thus, it is important that the investigator seek to balance the number of interviews between those who seek to raise issues and those who, given the opportunity, do not identify problems or positive aspects of the work environment.

As a matter of validity, it is generally recommended that a systemic investigation get input from between 10 and 20 percent of the specific employee population being studied, followed by interviews with a high proportion of supervisors and managers, many of whom will need to respond to specific or general issues raised by employees.

## Setting up a systemic investigation

Since a systemic investigation will touch so many people in an organization, an investigator will need to strategize on the way the investigation will be conducted. If allegations are extremely serious, and if true, suggest a high probability of suppression or retaliation, the investigator will need to consider a highly intensive investigative strategy, bringing in multiple interviewers over a short time period, as well as placing key leaders on administrative leave for the period the investigation is ongoing. Naturally, this is extremely disruptive to an organization but may be necessary when the stakes—as well as the risks—are high.

In most organizations, the need for stealth and urgency will be less significant than when investigating time-specific allegations, allowing the investigation to be conducted over time and while the normal course of business unfolds. This is best accomplished by ensuring that leaders know the investigation is occurring and issue a communication to employees that will normalize the process. This might take the form of a memorandum to employees stating that the organization has retained a consultant to look at work climate, explaining that as part of the work being done that some employees will be contacted for interviews, and instructing those contacted for interviews to cooperate, as well as offering the opportunity for any employee with a desire to do so to contact the consultant. This communication need not include the word "investigation," nor does it need to state the impetus for the investigation. In general, this type of proactive communication is better than simply allowing the process to unfold.

The notices provided in a systemic investigation should be carefully worded to alert those interviewed as to appropriate expectations for feedback from the investigation. It is appropriate to have a specific item in pre-interview notices that states the interviewee might not be entitled to any feedback from the investigation; instructions as to the importance of refraining from discussion should also be explicit and clear.

## Preparing questions for an investigation of systemic discrimination

Although every interview should begin with the most general questions possible, forming an inverted triangle from open-ended to specific, in most investigations, the investigator has a clear picture of what the subject of the specific questions are going to be. In a systemic investigation, the investigator must be prepared for a wide variety of eventualities, such as interviews that are relatively unproductive or those that uncover dramatic new information.

The scheme of questioning, therefore, should involve the creation of a set of topical questions that are completely open-ended and cover a variety of aspects of organizational life. Because it is preferable to facilitate an uninterrupted narrative, the best way to begin the interview is with an explanation that the investigator is interested in learning about the work environment as a whole, about how people are treated and about how people get along. An opening questions such as, "Tell me what it's like to work here," or "Describe your experience as an employee here," will often net some degree of narrative, which can be aided by neutral prompts. Because the investigator is not necessarily driving toward particular fact questions, however, the third stage of the interview will involve more novel probes than most interviews.

# Questioning framework for respiratory medicine clinic (samples)

## Questions for employees:

- How is it to work here? What do you like or not like about this place?
- How do people get along?
- How are you supervised? How do you know how you are doing?
- Have you had any concerns about how you or others were treated?
- On a scale from "extremely fair" to "extremely unfair," how would you describe the decisions that are made about people here, and why?
- Have you had any concerns about how and how much you are paid? Are you aware of any issues around pay or compensation?
- Who gets promoted here? What makes people valuable?
- Do you feel that you have the same opportunity to succeed as others? Why or why not?
- How do the staff and physicians get along here? Are you aware of any issues or problems? Have you been made aware of any problems among the doctors or the doctors and nurses?
- What hours do you work? Do you ever work extra hours? How is that handled?
- If you need or want to use your leave, is that ever a problem? How or why?

It will be up to the investigator as to which of these questions nets answers worth pursuing further, but there is great danger in not digging far enough. Pushing for incidents, details, witnesses, and times is important, and often requires assisting interviewees in thinking back over time or reviewing old documents and records.

"Everyone knows that it used to be bad for the Latinos here."

"Everyone?"

"Yeah, it was pretty much openly acknowledged that Latinos weren't going to get promotions."

"Openly acknowledged in what sense?"

"Oh, you know, supervisors would make comments."

"Can you be more specific?"

"Well, I don't remember any specific events, but Max—he was the supervisor in supply—he would say really intense things in front of managers, and no one would object."

"'Intense things'?"

"Yeah, like he once said in a meeting there weren't gonna be any Spanish-speakers bossing him around."

"Where did you hear him say that?"

"In a staff meeting in the conference room."

"Which managers were there?"

"I don't know—whatever managers we had at the time. Everyone had to attend."

"When was this?"

"A few years ago."

"It's pretty important that we try and nail down when this occurred. What was being discussed at the meeting?"

"Well, it was right before we moved..."

"...and the move was in June of 2002?"

"Yeah...like a month or two before."

"Okay, so maybe March or April of 2002 in the conference room, you heard Max make this statement?"

"Yes."

"And you are certain that managers were present?"

"Yeah, they were all there."

"And what were their responses to the statement?"

"Nothing. That's what surprised us all so much. They just completely let it go."

"Do you remember what prompted Max to make the statement?"

"Oh yeah, I remember they announced that a managerial job was opening up, and Eduardo Ramos said that maybe he'd apply."

"So did Max make this statement to Eduardo?"

"No, just kind of to the room."

Clearly after an exchange like this, there would be a need to probe as to whether the interviewee had observed Max or anyone else making similar statements, following up with a search for minutes from a meeting at that time that might list attendees or at least identify some attendees through the minutes. An interview with Ramos would likely be productive, as well as adding to future interviews a question as to whether individuals had heard culturally or racially based statements made in meetings or elsewhere.

## Special issues in evidence collection

Collecting records that show patterns of decision-making over time is essential, particularly when examining patterns of conduct and possible systemic discrimination. It is often beyond the expertise of an investigator to conduct the appropriate analysis of voluminous historical records (such as compensation, benefits, recruitment, and hiring and offer information). Seeking assistance and expertise to draw appropriate conclusions and make appropriate observations is helpful and necessary. The investigator will need to establish confidentiality agreements and contracts with those experts, and provide the experts redacted information to protect the identity of the organization and individuals as necessary. Any written reports provided by those experts should minimally be referred to in the final investigative report and certainly maintained intact within the investigative file.

In addition to official records, the investigator will often find it helpful to sample routine communications; for instance e-mails between leaders and key staff people, posts on internal or external bulletin boards, or even copy lists on important communications can net "unofficial" evidence of irregularities or inequities. The results of these searches should be included in a final analysis and report. It is as important to state as part of a summary or report, however, when such searches yield nothing irregular or suspect.

# The critical role of independence

Because systemic investigations can become protracted and often involve careful scrutiny of the principals in an organization, the investigator must establish and maintain a clear set of relationships with the organization. Most often, the individual commissioning the investigation will be a senior leader; however, because that leader's own leadership will be part of the investigation, the investigator should insist on a contact with some distance from the day-to-day operations of the organization. This can be legal counsel, central administration (i.e., corporate headquarters), or a board of directors or committee of a board of directors. Beginning an investigation without clarifying and affirming this reporting relationship will increase the likelihood of interference or confusion during the course of the investigation. The investigator should not only affirm that the lone communication that will take place regarding the investigation will be limited to the agreed-on person, but that updates will only include a summary of progress made and estimates of additional steps necessary to complete the investigation. The investigator should be very careful to avoid sharing interim impressions or premature conclusions during the course of the investigation, as these can trigger premature organizational responses, or should early impressions change, can reduce the credibility of the investigation.

Any attempts to circumvent or interfere with the investigation, or any attempts to influence the outcome of the investigation through anything but normal channels should be carefully documented, and should also be considered when reporting behavioral and cultural norms in the organization.

# Special considerations in making findings

In typical investigations, the investigator is mindful that organizations will need to make decisions about actions to be taken in response to findings. Thus, an investigator strives to draw the most accurate conclusions about specific incidents and actions of individuals. In systemic investigations, findings may be less specific—a frustration to those seeking to take disciplinary action but a source of aid to those looking to course-correct overall organizational functioning. It is therefore appropriate to identify trends and themes in organizational functioning, particularly when exploring historical detail.

After completing interviews with 100 people in the respiratory medicine department, the investigator reported that in the late 1990s there was an undisputed disadvantage for Latinos who attempted to advance from hourly positions to supervisory positions. The investigator provided the following basis for the conclusion; 12 Latino employees, including 2 former employees, reported that their applications for supervisory positions were repeatedly "lost" or "overlooked," and they were therefore never interviewed for positions for which they had applied. Human resources staff at the medical center during that time did not recall these events, and the only information in the employees' files was that they had applied for the positions but were not interviewed "at the discretion of the hiring manager." Three current leaders acknowledge that former colleagues, no longer with the medical center, spoke openly about the futility of Latinos attempting promotion.

Ten Anglo employees stated that it was "widely known" in the nineties that Anglos had an advantage over Latinos in promotion, although none could recall specifically how they had gotten that information. Several Latino employees indicated that they informed friends and relatives to refrain from applying for jobs at the medical center because of this "glass ceiling." The former head of human resources states that there was never any deliberate attempt to overlook Latinos in promotion but acknowledges that during the years 1995–2001, there were no Latinos promoted to supervisor positions despite their representing 24 percent of the workforce within the respiratory medicine staff. Asked to explain this, he responded that he recalls there were "closed door" expressions of concern about English language competency that affected promotional decision-making. He did not recall any specific managers refusing to interview or hire Latinos. He does acknowledge that there were no efforts made to encourage or assist Latinos in seeking supervisory positions.

This trend in perception and recall is important for the decision-makers to understand, even if no single event worthy of remediation or discipline can be identified.

# CHAPTER 14

# Practical, Ethical, and Legal Issues in Investigations

Although there are no standard codes of ethics that apply to the multidisciplinary function of employment investigations, there are certain situations and norms investigators should be prepared to address.

**Maintaining independence**: Whether external or internal, investigators will deal with various threats to the independence of their investigation. The independence of the investigation is one of its strengths, and investigators must show a good deal of courage at times to insist on freedom from interference. Some of the risks to independence include the following:

1.  *Inquiries or requests for updates during the investigation:* It is completely acceptable for an investigator to communicate to the decision-maker or whoever retained him or her the expected duration of an investigation, or broad information such as the number of witnesses the investigator has remaining to interview. Beyond these logistical concerns, however, an investigator should feel no duty to share information that is being learned, and certainly he or she should avoid sharing any impressions or opinions that may have been formed. Not only does

sharing information chip away at the neutrality and independence of the investigation, it may create a risk that premature impressions lodge in the mind of the decision-maker or other authority.

2. *Setting limits:* The independence of an investigation can be compromised by interference, such as when an investigator is told that he or she is not to speak with certain employees, that the investigation must be completed within a particular time period, or when the investigator is instructed on the order in which he or she must interview people. An investigator must insist on conducting the investigation in the manner he or she determines will accomplish the core purpose of an investigation: to determine "what happened," or "what is happening." Investigators need unfettered access to the organization in order to accomplish this in a straightforward manner. There may be one exception to this, however, when the need arises to interview nonemployees, such as clients or vendors. In order to avoid damaging the business interests of the organization, the investigator *may* agree to notify an appropriate party should such contacts be necessary to ensure that the contacts are handled with the proper discretion and diplomacy. This applies only when doing so does not in any manner exceed the strict "need to know" standard.

3. *Attempts to influence the outcome of the investigation:* It is not unheard of for a high-level leader of an organization to suggest or imply his or her expectations for the outcome of an investigation, and more rarely, to overtly state a preference as to the investigation's result. This is where an investigator truly must have fortitude and courage, as the appropriate response to this is to not only reiterate the independence and neutrality of the investigation, but to document such attempts in the credibility section of his or her report.

**Maintaining fairness:** Employment investigations must be even-handed and provide parties the opportunity to have their versions of events fairly considered. Furthermore, the process itself must be fair. To this extent, investigators need to consider certain behavior that might compromise the fairness of the investigation:

1. *Failing to allow a response:* No matter how persuasive a complainant might be, and no matter how damning the evidence appears, there is little to be lost and a great deal to be gained by allowing the accused to respond to the allegations prior to concluding the investigation.

   A custodian came to the human resources manager with a piece of the vice president of finance's letterhead in her hand. She explained that she had found this on the desk of one of the female finance employees. On the letterhead was a note that said, "I will love you forever. You are the best." Shocked, the HR manager brought the note to the attention of the CEO. The CEO immediately convened the board of directors to consider corrective action. It was days later when the VP of finance was able to explain, and for the female employee concur, that the employee's preteen daughter had come with her to work during the prior week and had been allowed to sit in the VP's office while he met with her mother. During this time, the daughter had used a piece of the VP's letterhead to write her mother a note.

2. *Using deception:* In employment investigations, investigators must carefully consider any use of deception from both legal and ethical perspectives. Perhaps the most prominent example of improper deception arises from visible corporate use of "pretexting," a rather elegant word for an investigator's lying about who he or she is in order to get information. When this tactic is used to attempt to gain access to someone's financial records, for instance, there is more than a small chance one

will run afoul of the law, or at least attract significant attempts to prove so.

In general, it is improper for those investigating internal employment matters to pretext. There may be exceptions, but they should be rare, compelling, and legally sound. This limitation does not preclude being vague about one's role at times ("I am doing a project for the Acme Corporation, and I'd like to get some information from you.") or refraining from volunteering one's role or purpose, particularly when dealing with those outside the organization.

A second form of deception that an investigator should use with extreme care is implying or suggesting that testimony or evidence has been received when, in fact, it has not. The most common use of this form of deception is the hypothetical.

Rhiannon denied stealing the bus passes from the office manager's desk. "Rhiannon," said the investigator, "what would you say if I told you three people indicated they actually saw you remove those passes from the desk?"

The deception here, of course, is that there are no such witnesses, and the interviewee may or may not know that. This can be a helpful way to provoke a more thoughtful answer from a respondent making denials, or to use during the fourth stage of a complainant or witness interview. Such questions, however, can backfire by rapidly eroding faith in the neutrality or integrity of the interviewer, and therefore should be used only when they can be defended as essential in attempting to reach a determination in a matter where the credibility of parties is at issue.

Finally, attorneys have special obligations under Rules of Professional Responsibility to be particularly careful to avoid misrepresenting their role when dealing with a party who is not represented by counsel:

"In dealing on behalf of a client with a person who is not represented by counsel, a lawyer shall not state or imply that the lawyer is disinterested. When the lawyer knows or reasonably should know that the unrepresented person misunderstands the lawyer's role in the matter, the lawyer shall make reasonable efforts to correct the misunderstanding."[1]

## Compliance with Section 7 of the National Labor Relations Act[2]

With some exceptions, such as the public sector and supervisory employees, the NLRA ensures that employees can discuss the "terms and conditions" of their employment. This limits the demands that an employer can place on an employee when instructing them to maintain the integrity of an investigation. Instructing an employee to "not discuss the subject of this investigation with anyone," for instance, may be a sufficiently broad instruction to give rise to concerns about interference with this right. To avoid this, the instructions to an employee should be narrow and specific:

> If anyone asks you about the content or subject of this interview, the proper response would be, "I have been instructed not to discuss it."

This instruction is of sufficiently narrow scope to avoid an appearance of restricting an employee's right to discuss overall work conditions with others.

---

[1] Rule 4.3,American Bar Association Model Rules of Professional Conduct
[2] 29 U.S.C. §§ 151–169

## Contacts after the investigation has been completed

For internal investigators, it is often inevitable that there will be incidental or even routine contact with parties once an investigation is complete. For external investigators, it is most likely that, absent a court appearance, there will be no contact with the subject of an investigation. Sometimes, however, parties to an investigation have experiences, concerns, information, or even admissions that they bring forward after the close of the investigation. For either an internal or external investigator, this requires caution and thoughtfulness.

**A party contacts the investigator to verify the findings of the investigation:** Sometimes a party who is unhappy with the outcome of an investigation will contact the investigator to find out if the results communicated to the party by the employer are the same results that the investigator actually presented. The best response to this will have been set up in the planning stages of the investigation by including in the notices checklist a statement that "once (the investigator) completes his/her report, she/he will only discuss that report with the employer." In that case, the investigator can simply refer the party back to that statement and clarify that he or she cannot release information on behalf of the employer. In any case, this is a request that an investigator cannot honor, no mater how tempting.

**A party contacts the investigator to provide new/ additional information**: When new information becomes available, an investigator has several safe choices—to refer the party back to the employer's complaint response system and to instruct them to bring it forward in that way, or to have him or her contact the decision-maker directly and to inform the decision-maker of the new information.

An investigator may, however, choose to inquire of the party as to whether he or she has information that is *more of* what was reported before, *different from* what was reported before, or *a change in* what was reported before. If the employee answers that it is the first or second option, the employee should then be instructed to report the behavior to the employer. If the answer is that this is a change in what had been reported before—in other words, possibly a retraction or a substantial enhancement—the investigator may choose to notify the employer him- or herself and decide if an interview is warranted to determine whether the investigation needs to be reopened.

**A nonparty contacts the investigator to provide new information:** Sometimes an employee will make a casual or a pointed reference to a problem he or she is having with someone who has been the subject of the complaint in the past. A respondent, hearing this, may tell the person to contact the investigator to describe the situation or the incident. In these circumstances, it is not appropriate for an external investigator to handle this information. It is appropriate for an internal investigator only if he or she clarifies that the conversation is a new intake, and that the person is being spoken to as a fresh complainant.

**A party who has been found by the investigation to have engaged in misconduct contacts the investigator with new information about the credibility of the complainant or witnesses:** The proper response to this kind of contact is to point out to the (former) respondent that the investigation is closed, but he or she is entitled to report to his or her employer if he or she believes a complaint was filed falsely or maliciously.

**A complainant who calls to retract his or her testimony:** Retractions in employment matters come for lots of reasons, not the least among them pressure to do so that comes from the organization. Nevertheless, since the investigation has been completed and action taken, the investigator should tread carefully, balancing inquiry with the reason for the retraction with clarity that the investigation has been closed. An external investigator, again, would want to communicate with the employer and seek direction. An internal investigator might evaluate the complainant's retraction and determine whether further inquiry was called for.

## Managing attorney-client privilege

Among the areas that should be addressed at the outset of an investigation is whether and how to maintain attorney-client privilege over material or communication. Generally, communication between attorneys and corporate agents on subjects relating to the attorney's representation are protected from compelled disclosure. In the course of an employee making a complaint or in the processing of how to respond to the complaint, there will usually be conversations that have legal consequences. Accordingly, one set of issues any organization should address is whether communications related to complaint processing should be protected.

Because attorney-client privilege requires an attorney to be part of the communication, and because the issues and implications are legal, the decisions should be made with the assistance of the organization's counsel. An investigator will often find him- or herself in uncertain waters if these privilege issues are not addressed at the outset.

Any decision to provide or preserve privilege will affect decisions as fundamental as how an investigator is identified. If privilege is to be preserved, it might be necessary for a lawyer—either in-house or external to the organization—to supervise or retain the investigator so it is clear from both documents and practice that the purpose of the investigator's activity is to assist the attorney in advising the organization. Such a decision will have obvious ramifications on the investigator's ability to maintain that he or she was hired as a neutral third party, regardless of how impartially the investigation is actually conducted. If the organization wants an investigation that more readily appears to a casual observer to be impartial, then there may be tough choices to make—and directives to issue—about forfeiting attorney-client privilege.

What is clear is that the investigator will need to know (a) whether all inside persons will speak candidly, and (b) whether the purpose of the investigation is to assist the lawyer or to make impartial findings of fact. Both objectives can be achieved only by the organization's first making certain decisions about privileged communication.

One area that is frequently overlooked—even when an investigator is hired to assist the attorney—is the availability of some of the investigator's material to other parties through "discovery." Discovery is a legal procedure by which one side to a conflict can obtain information about another side's case. Although the mental impressions of an investigator who is hired to assist the lawyer may be protected from discovery, the investigator's records of nonprivileged facts, such as what a witness says about the complainant's or respondent's conduct on a particular day, are not protected.

Consequently, it is prudent to keep one's facts separate from the impressions that one develops on the basis of those facts. If the investigator is keeping records on paper, the process can be relatively straightforward. But if the records are kept in a database used for investigative purposes, then care should be taken at the outset of the investigation to ensure that facts and impressions are coded distinctly and that the database can be redacted before being turned over to the other side pursuant to discovery.[3]

It should also be mentioned that even if an organization does retain an attorney to conduct an investigation in anticipation of litigation, if the timely and thorough nature of the investigation or the methodology of the investigation is to be asserted as a defense, the investigation itself becomes material and attorney-client privilege does not apply.

## Questions about needing a lawyer

An investigator should expect that a party learning for the first time that he or she is accused of wrongdoing will

---

[3] Note that under new procedural rules in the federal courts, which are widely adopted by states, digital information may be have to be disclosed in "native format," so that the database itself, not reports, are what is turned over.

ask the investigator whether they should obtain legal representation. The investigator should in all instances avoid suggesting that this is not an option or that the question itself is improper, while at the same time avoiding promotion of the interviewee's withdrawal. The proper response in this case is to let the interviewee know that the investigator cannot provide him or her with advice about hiring an attorney, but that this is simply a fact-finding interview, and that should misconduct be discovered, they would have every opportunity to seek counsel. Most interviewees will continue after this discussion, which should be carefully documented. If an employee insists on obtaining legal representation, it is best to allow a break in the interview to allow him or her to proceed with consulting an attorney. Of course, in most instances, that attorney will not be permitted to participate in the interview, and this should be made clear to the interviewee.

## Additional concerns for lawyers

Both the Rules of Professional Responsibility[4] and common sense suggest that attorneys should carefully consider serving as an investigator, and subsequently a possible witness in matters where they or a member of their firm are representing the employer:

> "The client is harmed if the lawyer's testimony contradicts that of the client or if the lawyer's credibility is impeached. The adversary is harmed by potential confusion of the jury as to the role of the lawyer/witness."[5]

---

[4] Rule 3.7, ABA Model Rules of Professional Responsibility
[5] Rosenblatt, Richard G, "Ethics and Privileges in the Context of Employment Investigations," Presented at the New Jersey Institute for Continuing Legal Education, 2003

# CHAPTER 15

# The Dynamics of a Harassment Complaint

A complaint is not a simple thing. By the time an employer has received a complaint of harassment or discrimination, a complex set of interpersonal and intra-psychic processes have coalesced to generate that complaint. In fact, a complaint of discrimination or harassment is the logical endpoint in an often-predictable pattern involving employee perceptions and expectations, employee dis-engagement, and organizational practices.

Every employer knows that complaints of harassment and discrimination are time-consuming, complex, and often disruptive. They involve tangled webs of complex issues. As a result of dealing with complaints that are messy and generally mired in interpersonal conflict, managers, human resources professionals and attorneys can become cynical about the motive and purpose of a complaint.

The perception of a complaint's validity is more than occasionally shaded by the complainant's prior conduct and performance, or by prior complaints he or she has made. Given a complainant's rocky employment history or turbulent relationships, a complaint may be viewed, on its face, as suspect. As a result of this perception, a paradox ensues: *the manner in which employers respond to complaints can result in escalation, rather than resolution, of the matter.* As an investigator, one cannot be drawn into similar thinking. The human tendency to prejudge is a dangerous one for a fact-finder. The best way to avoid such prejudice is to understand why those things that might appear to make a complaint less credible are, in fact, the things which, if not credibility enhancing, can at least be explained in a manner consistent with truth-telling.

Over nearly 20 years, Sepler & Associates has conducted informal and formal research into the thoughts, feelings, and experiences of individuals from the moment they recognize they have a problem until the time they make a complaint. I have further explored their decision-making once they choose to complain. Although chapter 3 focuses on the perceptions of a complainant, this chapter will discuss the psychological and organizational processes that are underway up until the time a person *becomes* a complainant.

A case to consider:

> Barbara Jones is employed by Redword, a Fortune 500 company. She has worked in the finance department for eight years, first in a clerical position and then in professional positions of increasing responsibility to the top nonmanagerial position as senior account representative. She is eligible for bonuses and has received modest bonuses each year. She received an achievement award in her third year of employment. Her performance reviews were unremarkable until the prior year, when she received several Ns (needs improvement).
>
> Barbara works in a group of eight employees—two male and six female—all of whom have been with the company five years or more. They report to James Alton, a career manager with Redword, who has supervised this group for 15 years. James is Caucasian. Barbara and two of her colleagues are African American. One colleague is an Asian immigrant. The rest are Caucasian.
>
> Barbara has filed a complaint of harassment and discrimination with Redword's human resources department.

She claims that there has been inappropriate (racially and sexually charged) humor used by her coworkers and between James and her coworkers—both male and female—for six years.

A recent selection of her coworker, Monica Sands, to attend a conference was based on James's preference for white employees; Barbara and one other African American employee were denied the opportunity to attend despite submitting requests to attend for three and two years, respectively.

James is harsher with Barbara and other African American employees in regard to errors and is more rigid in applying rules and regulations with African American employees than with the other employees. This has become worse during the past year, when James began documenting even her most minor infractions while ignoring the same infractions in others. James has asked Barbara inappropriate questions about her personal life, including asking about her dating life and evening activities.

While the investigation is ongoing, James has already contacted the investigator to ensure that she is apprised of the following:

- Barbara has recently been placed on a performance improvement plan (PIP) due to declining productivity and a lack of apparent willingness to make needed improvements. PIP employees are not eligible for out-of-state travel.
- Barbara has been written up for attendance issues three times in the past two years, and has been coached informally about disappearing from her work area. She has also been spoken to about time wasting and professionalism.
- Barbara was the subject of an informal complaint by two coworkers last year for being disruptive, and for excessive nonwork discussion. No record was made of the complaint and no action was taken. Instead, the coworkers rearranged their cubicles to minimize disruptions.

- Barbara has, until recently, been very open and forthcoming about her personal life. In fact, she has directed several coworkers and James himself to a blog she writes about her dating experiences, which includes some suggestive content.

Since Barbara filed the complaint last week, two coworkers have commented on feeling uncomfortable with her, stating she stares at them and makes hostile faces.

This case has several elements that point to some typical patterns and underlying dynamics of harassment cases:

- Reporting takes a long time (six years in this case).
- The complainant's own conduct or reaction to prior conduct makes claims of unwelcomeness suspect (in this case, the complainant discusses her dating life, suggesting that she may signal that she welcomes the very personal discussions about which she complains).
- Possible inappropriate conduct. (Is she writing the blog on work time? Is her discussing the blog with coworkers appropriate?)
- Performance and attitude issues (performance improvement, subject of prior complaints, and coaching regarding her own conduct).
- Relationship issues (coworkers have complained about her, and current issues with staring or making faces).

Since an investigator will encounter one or more of these dynamics when investigating harassment, discrimination, and other complaints, there are several key concepts and models that will be helpful to review in order to best deconstruct those dynamics when investigating complaints.

**Declining immunity**: Both the complainant-to-be and the ultimate respondents play a role in the extraordinary length of time it can take for someone to complain about workplace misconduct. The combination of habit and tolerance create a lethal incubation period that makes these cases particularly difficult to understand when conducting an investigation.

*Declining immunity* is a term that describes the human propensity to feel more and more troubled by conduct over time, despite the fact that the conduct has remained generally consistent. A simple way to explore this is by examining a typical marital situation *and* reacting to a spouse's or partner's habit:

> You are in love. Your heart flutters each time you think of your companion. You have a sense of wonder and excitement in your life, and you can barely concentrate on worldly matters as you delight in the new and wonderful relationship that is unfolding. The target of your affection is terrific. Everything about this person fascinates and attracts you—from his or her smile, to the way this person speaks, to his or her little eccentricities. You even think that funny way he or she sniffs when reading is adorable. Almost puppy-like, you think, how earnest this person is when reading, that he or she doesn't hear these little snorts. It is really adorable.

> Some time has passed now. The early stage of infatuation has become a less cataclysmic affection as you have settled into a more committed relationship. Yes, this person is still "the one," but real life has set in and occasionally small challenges arise. During this time, you realize that when you both sit together reading, as you so enjoy doing, the unconscious sniffing of your partner has become a bit distracting. It is such a small thing but probably worth nipping in the bud. "Darling," you say, "I love you so....but there is a tiny little problem I'd like to address with you." In the most loving and supportive way, you tell your beloved the sniffing distracts you, and you ask him or her to try to be more aware of it. Distressed at your distress, your partner apologizes and readily agrees, and for a period, your shared reading time is blissfully silent.

Now well into a settled relationship, it is several years later. Promises of "sniff awareness" have been made and broken, as your partner mindlessly and inconsiderately falls repeatedly back into a nasal cacophony as you read. You decided some time ago that it was simply not worth it to try and deal with the problem anymore, but instead have invested in noise-canceling headphones to wear as you sit in your side-by-side recliners reading. It really is not a lot of trouble, although you do resent having to be inconvenienced. Furthermore, if you were really honest about it you would admit that your partner's failure to address the behavior suggests a lack of respect, which makes you wonder how mutual your affection really is.

More time passes. One day, you sit down to read a wonderful novel and become absorbed. Soon, you hear your spouse enter the room. You glance over at the thick headphones, and something just snaps. You turn to your partner and say, "No way are you coming in here and ruining my quiet. I am sick to death of wearing those stupid headphones. I have had it with your lack of consideration and noisemaking. Either you go someplace else and read, or I am going to the library." Your partner is stunned. This is something completely unexpected. Why are you suddenly so oversensitive? It's just a little noise, and it's the same noise your partner was making when all was wonderful. Your partner suspects that this really isn't about the snorting at all, but is your attempt to pick a fight. After all, why didn't you say something if it was bothering you so much?

*Declining immunity* occurs when an individual has a high stake in a relationship. In the case of workplace misconduct, the person bothered by the conduct generally has a strong interest in maintaining his or her employment relationship (based on financial or psychological needs or a combination of both), and may also have a high stake in the relationship to the individual whose behavior is at issue. The greater the stake or interest in those relationships, the longer it may take for the unwelcomeness of the conduct to override those interests to the point that it becomes "worth it" to disrupt the relationship and complain about the conduct. In a surprising number of harassment cases, conduct that is presented to the employer as sufficiently disruptive to seriously affect the "terms and conditions" of someone's employment began as innocuous or welcome conduct, transforming over time in the mind of the complainant without any change in the behavior itself.

***Implications for investigators:*** As an investigator, understanding the process of declining immunity helps one to formulate questions about retrospective perceptions and prior interactions. An investigator can ask a complainant to describe if and how his or her perceptions changed over time, or whether he or she felt differently about the conduct in the past. Similarly, an investigator can examine whether changes in the relationship between the complainant and respondent were noted by others. Understanding the emotional "fraying" that occurs with continuous exposure to bothersome conduct can also prepare an investigator for strong emotion on the part of the complainant at the time of the primary interview.

# The question of intent

When studying the evolution of a complaint from the perspective of a complainant, the self-protective mechanisms that delay are relatively easy to grasp. It may be a bit harder to understand or even identify with an alleged bad actor, as most professionals in the workplace believe that violating work rules indicates some sort of intent or knowledge of wrongdoing. The reality is that most individuals who have been found to violate workplace conduct are not behaving in a targeted, malicious way; they are behaving habitually, without really contemplating the consequences of their behavior.

To be certain, there are "bad" actors who are power-based and intentionally harmful (particularly among high-earning professionals or "rainmakers"), and psychologically needy individuals who reach out inappropriately to have their emotional or psychological needs met (very often in concert with a life change such as divorce). But by some estimations, more than 60 percent of workplace harassment is neither needy nor power-based, but *ignorant or inadvertent.* To be very effective in investigating workplace misconduct, an investigator should be familiar with the mindset of this type of possible bad actor. From his or her standpoint, the conduct at issue may be undisputed, but he or she is completely unclear why the conduct is a problem. Conversely, this person may simply be unaware of the conduct, as well as the degree to which the conduct has upset the complainant.

> Morgan has complained about division director Taylor's repeated invitations to go out on a date. Morgan reports refusing these invitations repeatedly and Taylor becoming more and more insistent. After five invitations, Morgan believes Taylor is simply attempting to intimidate by continuing to make these requests for dates.
>
> After getting over the initial shock at being the subject of a complaint, Taylor acknowledges inviting Morgan to dinner, stating that when they are both working late, he believes Morgan might think it rude if Taylor went to dinner without extending an invitation. Furthermore, Taylor notes that Morgan is shy and does not want that to stand in the way of an opportunity to develop a relationship with an organizational leader.
>
> Although Morgan insists that Taylor's invitations were thinly veiled requests for a date, Taylor adamantly insists that they were nothing but polite invitations to share a meal.

Whether the conduct occurred the way it was perceived by a complainant or the way it was intended and perceived by the respondent becomes a focus of many investigations. This "disconnect" can be even more challenging when a complainant insists he or she objected to behavior, while the person to whom the objection was made has no recall of such an objection or disputes the specificity or clarity of the objection.

Charles insists that he had repeatedly objected to Miranda's inappropriate remarks and that Miranda had disregarded the objections. Miranda indicated that Charles would roll his eyes and laugh when she made such comments and he once told her she was "naughty," but she never understood he seriously objected to the language, which she still believes was inoffensive and appropriate.

This characterization points out an important dynamic of much workplace misconduct—that rather than being *targeted and intentional*, it is just as likely to be *habitual*. A useful analogy in this instance compares rules in the workplace with rules governing car travel. Just as work policies are clearly written in black and white, so are the speed limits posted on public roads. Despite the clarity of posted speed limits, and the clear understanding by drivers that violating those speed limits can result in serious consequences, it is estimated that more than 70 percent of licensed drivers violate the posted speed limit at least once each month. What is it that drivers are thinking to allow this rate of noncompliance? The answers one hears will be familiar to anyone who has addressed workplace misconduct:

"Everyone else was doing it."

"No one ever said anything before."

"A lot of people go faster than I was going."

"The speed limit wasn't well posted."

"It's a dumb speed limit for this big of a street."

"Everyone else does it," "No one objected," and "I wasn't hurting anyone" are common refrains when someone is confronted for violating a workplace policy. What they mask is that in most cases until the person was pulled over, he or she probably had given little consideration to his or her behavior. Violations become so routine or mindless they become second nature to the violator. This is why the first question a police officer will ask an alleged speeder is, "Do you know the speed limit here?" followed by, "Do you know how fast you were driving?" The response is usually an embarrassed shrug of the shoulders. Habitual speeders and habitual policy violators are defensive or at least surprised when being confronted about their behavior because they are habitually, and often mindlessly, doing what they have been doing for years.

*Implications for investigators:* The implications of the "habitual" nature of extensive misconduct are extremely important for an investigator, particularly when interviewing a person accused of misconduct. Those who attempt to "squeeze confessions" or obtain "admissions" from alleged bad actors, or who confront people with questions about "misconduct" or "violations of policy" will often net poor results. It is difficult to extract an admission of wrongdoing from someone who not only does not believe he or she has done wrong but may not even be aware of the behavior in question. Behaving in an adversarial way or using criminal-type interrogation techniques will only amp up claims of innocence. This and other interviewing implications are discussed in chapter 8.

# Full cups, thin skulls, and stress theory

Another factor to consider in understanding how complaints emerge is the coping capability an individual brings to the workplace. In civil law, there is a doctrine known as "the thin skull doctrine," which suggests that when someone is harmed due to a particular vulnerability because of negligence or intentional acts, it does not make those responsible for the harm any less liable. If two people are both hit by bricks falling from a construction site, and one suffers a mild concussion while the other is killed because of a congenital thinness of her skull, the construction company should not be able to argue that the companion's survivors are owed only for the damage they and she would have suffered had she not had the congenital anomaly. The implication of this doctrine is that, when determining damage, one is to "take them as they are," rather than substitute a median sample. To this end, we must consider that individuals come to the workplace with varying histories and related vulnerability or resilience.

People come to the workplace with a wide variety of sensibilities. Ten people hearing the same off-color joke in the workplace may respond 10 different ways. Some will not even notice that the joke was off-color. Some will find it offensive but blow it off. Some will find it hilarious despite of or because of its off-color nature, and others will be deeply offended. The outward response will range from laughter to eye rolling to silence to confrontation. If we "take each person as we find him or her," we must consider that *reasonable people will vary widely in the degree of tolerance they have for a particular situation and will demonstrate different behaviors in response to unwelcome conduct.* Add the growing disenchantment with behavior discussed as "declining immunity," and investigators should expect that there is no "typical" expression of distaste or "standard" degree of tolerance for inappropriate conduct.[1]

To understand variance in coping capability, it is helpful to think of unwelcome workplace behavior as a form of *stress.* By definition, stress is a reaction by an individual to forces from the outside world. In the real world, we deal with many single incidents and situations that create stress every single day. Employees might deal with a difficult customer, struggle with a problem they can't readily solve, or worry about the status of an ongoing project. Each of these instances is a single "drop" of stress each person carries in his or her individual psyche—and

---

[1] Although most organizations have policies that define harassment as it is described in law—as unwelcome conduct—investigators should determine whether the organization in which the conduct being investigated took place also has a policy prohibiting "inappropriate" conduct, which is not necessarily unwelcome.

just like a cup that collects liquids, each person's "mental container" has a capacity to carry a finite amount. Too much and one "overflows"; not enough, and one loses a sense of purpose.

Given the balancing act between too much and too little stress, people try to live their lives in a state of variable *equilibrium.* Depending on one's fundamental constitution, social support systems, personal history, and other things, people choose lives and careers that stimulate but don't overwhelm. Although everyone has his or her own "cup," there is no standard issue size. Joe may have a huge bucket while John has a container as small as a shot glass. Joe can handle immense amounts of stress without it affecting him, and John gets rattled fairly easily. Most agree that the world would be a far less worthy place without both sensitive Johns and thick-skinned Joes. Neither is inherently good nor inherently bad. They are simply different in their stress tolerance, and both are reasonable. Regardless of people's individual capacity, when their stress level accumulates to a high intensity and their "cup" begins to fill up, they get signals from their body that action is needed. These cues vary considerably—from mild changes in appetite and sleep patterns to more dramatic somatic issues, to cognitive cues like distraction, to emotional distress. *When life issues, work issues, or world events cause too much stress, the resources usually devoted to productive enterprises are rerouted to cope with the stress.*

While some periods of stress are normal, failing to cope effectively with cumulative or intense stress can result in serious problems in our work and relationships. Depending on the intensity and severity of the stress sources, coping may be as simple as counting to 10 or as difficult as sorting through deep grief. The degree to which our productivity is affected will also vary. To complicate things, while one stress source might seem trivial or small, its impact might be confounded by several other stress sources also at work; thus, a seemingly minor stress source can cause an irrationally strong reaction when it is viewed as part of a shower or flow of stress rather than just in the context of the single "drop" into the glass. If workplace misconduct, mistreatment, or discrimination is happening around us, our reaction will vary depending how full our "cup" might already be. Remembering that the human goal is to keep stress from becoming debilitating, the person feeling unhappy in the workplace faces a paradox. Nearly every person with a problem perceives that *reporting a problem itself is a form of stress.*

Keeping in mind the interest in relationships that underlie workplace functioning, the consideration of whether to bring a problem to the attention of an employer is a choice predicated on the expectation as to whether making such a report will make things more or less stressful.

> Ken likes his coworker Jenny and depends on her to help out when things get busy. He is an affable guy and doesn't get fazed much. Her occasional racial slurs bother him a lot, but he doesn't want to get her in trouble, and he needs her cooperation. Although he might provide her with subtle cues, or even direct feedback, his likelihood of reporting her is extremely low, until or unless he finds his ability to cope with her behavior compromised (e.g., perhaps he hears her use the slur in front of an equally valued Asian coworker) or his "immunity" declines (over time, tolerating the behavior becomes less and less acceptable, and he finds himself avoiding her, feeling resentful, etc).

It is not always fondness or maintenance of positive relationships that causes a delay in reporting.

> Karen is devastated by the sexual advances her director made toward her on a recent road trip. But she knows she is only a junior employee and the company will never believe her over him. Therefore, she tries to put the incident behind her, and move on.

> Douglas's residency has been plagued by the gross racial discrimination of the staff physician to which he has

been assigned. Douglas knows, however, that this physician is one of only five American experts in his subspecialty, and raising the issue will certainly put his career to a halt.

Roslyn has confronted Fred, the director of human resources, about his failure to address the conduct of an executive. "Roslyn," says Fred, "I would advise you to turn around, go back to your office, and forget the whole thing, lest you find yourself being charged with defamation."

It is not unheard of to find people who have been told convincingly that if they report an incident or problem, they will be ruining someone's career, or that their own career or reputation will be placed in jeopardy. Given these scenarios, it is easy to understand why some choose to continue to devote energy to coping rather than complain. Of course, coping means that one's "cup" continues to fill, and no matter how large the cup, there is no such thing as infinite capacity.

Depending on an individual's capacity to deal with stress and the effectiveness of their individual coping mechanisms, it is a certainty that stress will affect productivity. In a spiraling of negativity, the consequences of decreased social and work productivity will be more stress (poor performance reviews, family problems, conflicts, withdrawal from support networks), and their "cup" will finally reach a point where it is completely full. At that point, the cup begins to overflow; there is simply no more energy or capacity to cope. This is when an employer will receive the type of complaint described as a "charge" in the intake section, or it is the point where the individual will quit his or her job or take a leave of absence, often disability leave.

*For those reasons, investigators must explore the historical roots of a problem rather than just the event itself.* Too often, investigators will assume that because a complainant did not report conduct right away, there is some dissemblance occurring or the credibility of the complainant is lacking. Asking an individual what he or she did to deal with the behavior is both a helpful and informative query. This is particularly important in the investigator's essential mission to determine if misconduct occurred and if it was welcome or unwelcome. An investigator should take heed of the legal standards applied in harassment cases, which acknowledge that voluntarily tolerating or submitting to conduct does not signify that it is necessarily welcome. Discerning whether tolerating conduct is plausibly involuntary is very much a part of the job of an investigator. Differences in authority, status, and power are among the most common dynamics found in cases involving voluntary but unwelcome submission to inappropriate requests or demands.

In early research to try and understand the experience of becoming a workplace complainant, it became clear that some people come to the workplace with a "cup" that is already heavily loaded. One trend that emerged early on was the high correlation between individuals who went outside the workplace with their complaints (i.e., to the EEOC or state human rights authorities, or brought civil lawsuits) and a history of sexual victimization. Although 25 percent of those individuals who resolved their complaints without bringing outside charges reported a history of sexual victimization[2], a stunning 85 percent of those who brought charges reported such a history. Even though the correlation is merely a statistical relationship, it seems safe to conclude that a history of sexual victimization can make workplace conduct more readily perceived as stressful, and may in fact increase the distress experienced by unwelcome workplace conduct.

Thus, while Janet—without a history of victimization— might cope with the boorish behavior of a coworker by ignoring the conduct or making light of it, Deborah—with a history of abuse or victimization—might find herself reliving prior discomfort, pain, or trauma and become far less able

---

[2] Although this number may seem high, it appears to match up with the norms for American females cited by the National Resource Center on Child Sexual Abuse, which, after conducting the largest retrospective study to date on the frequency of child sexual abuse, reports that approximately 27 percent of those women have such histories.

to find helpful coping mechanisms. The implication is that Deborah might complain sooner in a more dramatic way. Or conversely, if Deborah has a history of being disbelieved about prior trauma, she might assume she is to blame for the conduct and repress reporting until the situation is intolerable. The relationship between a history of victimization and workplace claims is ripe for further exploration.

For the purposes of using this information to increase investigative effectiveness, however, these findings have serious implications, the most important being that *the intensity of a person's reaction to workplace conduct may be less a function of how objectively problematic the conduct is than the level of overall stress in the recipient.* Therefore, investigators must carefully explore the context in which conduct occurs and remain steadfastly neutral despite powerful emotions and reactions by a complainant. Similarly, a person who is stoic and unemotional when describing horrific acts may be using disassociation as a coping skill, particularly if he or she has been exposed to similar acts in the past.

In summary, a person who begins to scream and cry when a dog approaches does not reliably tell an observer whether the dog is dangerous, so much as that the person who is reacting powerfully might have a history of being attacked by a dog. A good investigator understands and elicits both the rationale of the complainant for being upset or offended, and the actual behavior of the respondent that elicited that reaction.

## The employee issue triad

Understanding possible psychological reasons for delayed reporting, or a long incubation period, can help to shed light on the frequency with which organizations find performance problems paired with complaints of harassment or discrimination. Barbara Jones, discussed at the beginning of this chapter, complained that for six years she tolerated inappropriate humor and that for at least a year she believed she has been treated poorly based on race; she appears to be complaining based on a recent denial of a request to attend a conference (her "cup" overflowing). In that case, the first disclosure made by Barbara's supervisor is that she is on a PIP. Although there are no studies that have declared the exact frequency with which complainants are also viewed as employees with "performance problems," it is extremely common. If one stops to consider the psychological process of enduring what one perceives as a negative or hostile or discriminatory work environment, as discussed earlier in this chapter, it is almost intuitive this would be the result.

Investigators will find that many complainants have entered "the employee issue triad," composed of *attendance problems, attitude problems,* and *work quality problems.* In other words, they will be under scrutiny for their failure to arrive on time or overuse of sick leave, they may have been disciplined for poor behavior or attitude, and their actual performance may have declined. Why is this so common?

Consider the following scenario:

> Mason comes each day to a job that feels less and less comfortable. She does not believe that people care about her, and every day she is forced to listen to language that she finds more and more objectionable. As a result of her discomfort, she has avoided being in groups, and because of her increasing withdrawal from social interaction, people have started to respond by automatically excluding her from invitations and work-related conversations.
>
> Mason has been arriving at work late and leaving early, and at times she disappears from her work area. Feeling unliked and alone, Mason spends a good deal of the day on the phone and instant messaging with her sister, who supports her and encourages her to look for another job. Mason has been talked to about coming late and knows she could lose her job if she doesn't start coming in sooner, but she hates her situation and is starting to just not care.

Not all employees who feel unhappy with their work situation become poor performers or develop attendance problems, but even the toughest eventually experience some deterioration in their productivity or ability to function through adversity.

Gabe, a young Latino man, had recently been recruited as assistant plant manager at an assembly plant located in a rural Midwestern area. Upon his arrival, he was immediately subjected to hostile and intense racial harassment by workers. His master's diploma, which hung on his office wall, was defaced. His car was vandalized. His picture from the newsletter was cut out and pasted on to a Mexican cartoon character's face and posted around the plant.

A proud and determined Gabe resolved to continue to work as the investigation unfolded, even though harassment was ongoing. On the day he was to be interviewed, however, he did not appear until one hour after the scheduled time. Asked why he was late, he responded by telling the investigator that he had gotten into his car to drive the plant and had been struck with such a violently ill feeling, he simply could not drive. "I could not will my hand to turn the key," he said, "and I found myself sobbing in my driveway."

One can imagine an individual with fewer internal resources than Gabe, and in a position of less authority, feeling too, that he simply "couldn't go there" on a particular day.

Similarly, if one is distressed with the conduct of others in the workplace, the distress is rarely isolated to the alleged bad actors. If one is being subjected to discrimination or harassment, then others are perceived as either collusive or at least cold and uncaring. It is common to hear complainants tearfully describe how no one raised a finger to help them—to state that "everyone knew, but no one said or did anything." This sense that others are allowing one to be harmed, or may even promote and participate in the harm, can quickly result in deteriorating workplace relationships. As one's stress level climbs, or "cup" fills, adaptive behavior might include passive aggression, withdrawal, expressions of hostility and resentment, or a lack of cooperation with those perceived to be part of the problem. Depending on the nature of the individual involved, this can rise to a level where corrective action or coaching occurs and can also result in disciplinary action, especially when coupled with performance problems.

If one is having attendance issues and attitude problems, the slide into actual work quality problems is nearly inevitable. The stress of the perceived harassing or discriminatory situation, the feelings of isolation and resentment, deteriorating relationships with coworkers and supervisors, and increased energy devoted to dealing with all of the above are certain ingredients for inattentiveness to detail, carelessness in production, or apathy toward results. The decreased performance may not be addressed in a timely way, as too many businesses allow supervisors and managers to wait for an annual performance review to deliver negative feedback. It is not uncommon for this performance review, resulting in a PIP, probation, or even termination, to be the catalyst for a report—the event that "filled the cup to the brim."

The question is whether it should be considered that poor performers will concoct harassment as a strategy to keep their jobs when they know they are in performance trouble. Any experienced investigator will tell you this is certainly a possibility when you see the "double bubble" of harassment complaint and performance problems. But they will also tell you that one cannot make assumptions about which is the chicken and which is the egg in this circumstance. As a result, it is highly recommended that *all personnel actions such as terminations, transfers, demotions, and suspensions are put in abeyance pending the outcome of an investigation.*

Of course, the investigation should include all factors that gave rise to the current situation. If it does turn out that the complaint is false or exaggerated[3], the action can be reinstated; if not, the employer will need to consider whether the course of action planned should be altered or withdrawn. Documentation is at the core of assuring that whatever action is taken is legitimately based on performance, and is not in any way retaliatory toward the complainant for making a report in good faith, if this is the case.

In summary, the three parts of the investigative triad are as follows:

1.  *Attendance issues,* which can be the natural outcome of an increasing aversion to the workplace. If the capacity to cope with the workplace is compromised, the self-preserving option is to seek distance. This can take the form of intermittent "disappearances"— early departures or late arrivals, or extensive time spent on breaks—or actual absenteeism.

2.  *Attitude issues,* which develop when an individual who feels targeted or victimized resents the insensitivity or perceived indifference of the organization and his or her peers. They can also arise from perceptions of favoritism or antagonism. The increasing tension experienced through coping may come out in "sideways" negativity or manifest itself as withdrawal or sullenness. Alliance formation and "clique wars" also are common as the complainant seeks support and demands that individuals declare their loyalties.

3.  *Work quality issues* are the inevitable result of attendance and attitude issues not attended to or resolved. Since some organizations follow a practice of progressive performance management, often with protracted corrective action plans, these issues can be sustained for a significant period of time.

---

[3] Not all complaints not supported by fact are malicious. Claims can be (a) maliciously false, involving fabricated events or gross misstatements of fact, (b) a complaint made in good faith that reveals a problem that does not rise to the level of a harassment or discrimination charge, or (c) good faith allegations that are indeterminate or unproven.

## Cultural conflict avoidance

The final dynamic investigators must understand about complaints involves the possible "welcomeness" of the conduct, or similar misconduct by the complainant. For example, it is so common as to be predictable that when being asked to conduct an investigation, the referring professional is anxious to have him or her know that the complainant "is no angel." These characterizations may be based on subjective impressions or actual observations of the complainant, or they may be based on suspicions that have arisen because the complainant appeared to enjoy the conduct until recently. Often the question will be raised, "If he didn't like it, why didn't he tell them to stop?"

There are several threads to follow when faced with suggestions that the complainant "egged on" or at least failed to discourage the behavior that is now alleged to be unwelcome. One, of course, was that the complainant was not initially or even eventually offended by the conduct and is only raising the conduct at this time for self-interested reasons. There are other explanations that should be considered as well, particularly in light of all of the psychological adaptation described earlier in this chapter. Recalling the reasons that people do not report, we find similar reasons why they go along with or fail to object to conduct. In Sepler & Associates' research, the three reasons people gave for failing to verbally object to conduct included affiliation, fear, and cynicism:

"I didn't want to hurt his feelings."

"I figured if I said anything, it would only get worse."

"I thought he'd fire me."

"I tried to be subtle, but she just didn't get it."

"I tried to say something, but no one listened."

"It wouldn't do any good."

"If you let them know it bothers you they only pile it on higher."

"I thought it was important to get along on a day-to-day basis, and it wasn't worth wrecking that by saying something."

These statements are likely familiar to those who work with interpersonal problems in the workplace. In considering such statements, one might also notice that the most apparent answer to the question, "Why didn't you say something?" is "In American culture, we generally *don't* say something." We tend to take a quick calculus of the possible outcomes of a confrontation, and generally decide that it is not "worth it."

Imagine that you have just taken your seat near the window as you prepare to fly to New York from Chicago. It has been a long day, and you are tired and looking forward to the chance to read the novel you bought in the airport. As you sit down, the person next to you begins to ask you questions about your trip, your business, and your family. What do you do?

Chances are that your answer to this question is not "I tell them to shut up and leave me alone." No; you are more likely to indicate that you would send subtle but hopefully clear nonverbal signals that you find the discussion unwelcome. You might break eye contact at the end of an answer; pull out your book and attempt to turn your attention to it; answer the questions in short, clipped answers; or look at your watch (a curious, but common signal that you "don't have time" for the conversation). Most seatmates would respect these signals, and although you might have to renew them occasionally, you would have rebuffed the unwelcome behavior in a careful and polite way. However, once in a while, we get those seatmates who aren't as sensitive as we'd like. Despite our clear nonverbals, they continue to chat. Now what?

Although those of us who fly frequently might say, "I'm sorry, I have a book I'd really like to read," in reality most people would abandon their reading time and continue the conversation. Among the hundreds of micro calculations that would transpire (our fundamental values, a range of goals we might have set for ourselves, our aspirations) would be an evaluation of the joy of reading versus the discomfort of upsetting or insulting the seatmate. Several hours captive next to a sullen or hurt seatmate would, for many people, be less objectionable than benign and maybe even interesting conversation, and so the decision would be made that *going along with the unwelcome behavior was more attractive than confronting it.* Now, if failing to address neutral behavior with a perfect stranger is difficult, imagine the added challenges of addressing highly charged behavior with someone whose cooperation you desire or who may sign your paycheck. Until the cumulative stress of tolerating the conduct became intolerable, going along might seem like an adequate strategy.

How do we know this conduct is actually cultural? If you got off that flight and went to baggage claim, and there you ran into a friend of yours, you might roll your eyes and say you had a bit of a headache. "I sat next to a fellow who didn't stop talking between Midway and LaGuardia," you would explain. If your "going along" with the unwelcome behavior was abnormal, your friend might ask, "Why didn't you tell them to leave you alone? Why didn't you ask to have your seat changed?" But in all likelihood, your friend would most likely say something like, "Oh, I hate when that happens," and then go on to tell you a story of something similar he or she experienced recently. This reinforcement of norms is a hallmark of culturally determined conduct. Your friend would be validating the cultural norm, and then reinforcing it by telling you about his or her similar observation of the norm.

What happens when the cultural norm of tolerating conduct comes up against the need to address that conduct? Although some complainants remain passive, others will try to "'work around" the norm by using subtle communication. The result is that in many cases complainants will tell you they have objected to the conduct, but they were not taken seriously, or the behavior abated for a time but then reemerged. It is important to ask the complainant to tell you exactly how he or she expressed discomfort or communicated that conduct was unwelcome. It is surprising how often the complainants will describe extremely subtle or "sideways" communications that could easily be missed or mistaken by the person to whom the communications were directed.

> Rhonda was a receptionist at a television station in a major city. She liked her job and the flexibility it provided her as a mother of small children. Her only objection was that Jeff, her boss, would constantly comment to her about the appearance of women, particularly younger women in the office. She found these comments crude and unprofessional. She told the investigator that she had repeatedly tried to get Jeff to stop making the comments, but he persisted. "I told him the comments weren't okay," she repeated several times. The investigator said to Rhonda, "Rhonda, why don't you act as though I am Jeff and say to me exactly what you said to him." Rhonda turned to the investigator and smiled. "I said, 'Jeff, that's not how you talk to a mommy.'" The investigator noted that Rhonda continued to smile as she made the statement, and more significantly, that in the middle of the sentence, she gave a big wink. When asked if she actually winked when speaking to Jeff about the behavior, she seemed confused. "Wink?" she asked. "I didn't wink." The investigator now had a different picture of the repeated "confrontations" described by Rhonda.

Investigators must ensure that they do not make assumptions about the clarity or directness of objections that are reported to them, nor should they assume that failing to confront the conduct signaled welcomeness. This once again reinforces the importance of evaluating whether conduct was welcomed or if it was voluntarily tolerated but still unwelcome.

In addition to a failure to confront conduct, investigators will also get information or reports that the complainant has "given it as good as they've gotten," or that they laughed along with or enjoyed the conduct. In some cases, this is absolutely the case and must be considered from an analytic perspective as well as figured into a credibility assessment (see chapter 9).

Maura was an administrative employee on the trading floor in a high-intensity financial company. She was a bit older than many of the traders but was well known for her toughness and salty sense of humor. This served her well in an environment where millions were made and lost in the space of minutes, tempers ran high, and language was hot. As thick-skinned as anyone, Maura would snap back at brokers who swore at her and chastise those who got overly crude.

Following an annual company offsite, Maura failed to appear for work, and at the end of the day, the firm received notice that Maura had hired an attorney and was filing a complaint of sexual harassment. The written complaint, received the next day, outlined a set of allegations that went back over several years, including allegations of inappropriate sexual conduct in the workplace between coworkers and supervisors, and highly explicit sexual pranks. It included copies of massive amounts of profane and sexual e-mails allegedly sent by traders to Maura over a period of three years. When the manager of the floor was told that a complaint had been filed and an investigation would commence, he deduced that the complainant was Maura and told the investigator that at the recent offsite, Maura had become extremely intoxicated and had offered to do a striptease for some of the traders. He indicated that he intervened and attempted to escort Maura to her room to "sleep it off," but that as she turned to go, she shouted out repeatedly, "But I want to show them my boobs!" He states that several traders had come to him over the years to express discomfort with Maura's innuendos, such as responding to a request by saying, "If I'm nice to you, will you be nice to me?" while licking her lips and making lascivious gestures.

Employment investigators will recognize that what had initially been a series of allegations has now become contextually more complex, and the investigation now includes possible misconduct on the part of the complainant, as well as exploring questions as to how the previous complaints had been documented or addressed, and specific questions about conduct at the recent offsite. It does not, however, eradicate or diminish the importance of fully investigating all of the allegations in the initial complaint and considering whether in each case the behavior occurred and whether it was welcome.

At the time of a complaint, an employee may have a history of tolerating, going along with, or even initiating specific statements or behaviors that appear complicit. Complainants will most frequently justify these as a function of attempting to maintain workplace relationships, build affiliation, and reduce conflicts. Generally, they will make a distinction between their own behavior and the objectionable behavior in terms of degree, intensity, explicitness or severity, frequency, and degree of unwelcomeness. It is the fact-finder's task to determine objectively whether those distinctions are accurate and to remain open to all possibilities.

APPENDIX A

# Intake Form

# Intake Protocol—Action Log (Page 1)

*This form should be faxed to the investigative coordinator, and case conference should be recorded on the reverse side of the original.*

Intake Manager _____ Date _____ Time _____

First Contact:

| | |
|---|---|
| _____ Telephone | Complainant Name _____ |
| _____ In person | Position _____ |
| _____ Written<br>    communication | Branch/department _____ |
| _____ Other | Telephone _____ PVM? Y N |

| | |
|---|---|
| How does the employee describe the issue or problem? | |
| How long has the issue or problem been going on? | |
| What prompted the employee to bring this forward today? | |
| Who has witnessed (W) or participated (P) in the situation? | |
| Briefly note specific incidents described to you, including when and where they occurred. | |
| Has the employee taken any steps to try to address the problem? What steps? | |
| Has this situation been previously reported to a supervisor or manager? If yes, when? | |
| How is this matter currently affecting the employee? Can he or she comfortably return to work? | |

# Intake Protocol—Action Log (Page 2)

*To be completed by HR or investigative coordinator in collaboration with supervisor.*

Date Received by IC_____ Contact Name _____
Date of Case
Conference _____ ID those on call _____

Action plan:

1. Interim actions

2. Additional fact-finding/discussion

3. Problem-solving strategy

4. Support provided

5. Other actions

Actions Taken          Parties Involved       Date /Time

# Notices Checklist

## Pre-Interview Checklist

Name of Witness _____

Ira Investigator has reviewed the following with me, and I understand the following:

- ☐ This interview is being conducted as part of an investigation into allegations of conduct or conditions that may violate the policies of Widget Companies.
- ☐ He has been retained by Widget Companies and will be making a report to them regarding her findings.
- ☐ That he is not and will not be authorized to discuss her findings with anyone else.
- ☐ He is serving as a neutral fact-finder, and has no preference or predetermined outcome.
- ☐ He will be taking notes, and these notes will remain in Ira Investigator's possession unless a court orders otherwise.
- ☐ I am participating voluntarily in this interview and may refuse to answer any questions.
- ☐ Although every effort will be made to preserve my privacy, information will be shared if it is necessary in order to conduct a thorough investigation.

□ Because it is the policy of Widget Companies to protect the privacy of all involved, I should not discuss this interview with any employee of Widget Companies or its business partners, vendors, or contractors.

□ If this investigation reveals a violation of Widget Companies' policies, the individuals who have violated those policies could be subject to discipline up to and including discharge.

□ Reprisal or retaliation against anyone who participates in this investigation is prohibited, and will be responded to promptly and remedially.

Signature _____ Date _____

# Three C Triage Overview

## The Three C's – Triage Model

### Contact—72 hours

| | |
|---|---|
| Complainant states: | Unaffected |
| | Observed only |
| Complainant reports: | Sole known incident |
| | Inexplicit or moderated in offensiveness |
| | Easily verifiable |
| Examples: | Distasteful joke told at public meeting |
| | Sexist comment made to individual or group |
| | Inappropriate social behavior at company function |

*Where the complainant is saying he or she is not currently uncomfortable or at risk.*

---

### Concern—48 hours

| | |
|---|---|
| Complainant states: | "Need help" |
| | "Have problem" |
| Complainant reports: | Second incident of contact level conduct |

| | |
|---|---|
| | Ongoing, subtle concerns |
| | Distraction or impact on performance |
| | Concerns about escalating conflict *(May demand confidentiality)* |
| Examples: | Ongoing sexual joke-telling |
| | Series of moderately offensive acts by colleague |
| | Dispute or tension with manager with possible gender-based overtones |
| | Fresh issue of work assignment, allocation of resources, favoritism |

*Where the complainant is oriented toward problem resolution: "I just want it to stop."*

---

## Complaint—immediate

| | |
|---|---|
| Complainant states: | File a complaint |
| | Being harassed or discriminated against |
| | Can't take it anymore |
| Complainant reports: | Physical contact |
| | Repeat of concern level conduct |
| | Disputed facts |
| | Highly explicit conduct or language |
| Examples: | Quid pro quo or consent issues |
| | Highly offensive statements |
| | Threats—overt or subtle—to safety or security |
| | Conduct reported to management and not responded to |

*Where the complainant is overwhelmed and highly distressed: "I can't take this anymore."*

# Sample Request to Preserve Documents

October 1, 2007

Marvin Manager
Acme Widget Corporation
333 Main Street, E
Yourtown, MN 51628

Dear Mr. Manager:

As you know, you have retained this firm to conduct an investigation into allegations brought forward by employees and by their union representatives.

In order to move this investigation forward, we will need to examine a variety of records that may be retained within corporate data storage or may be maintained on site. A list of the records we are requesting is attached to this letter.

During the course of this investigation, we ask that you, in your corporate role, instruct your own Human Resources staff and ensure that the managerial and supervisory staffs at the North Dakota, Western Ohio, and East Tennessee sites are instructed to preserve any and all documents that may pertain to the management of personnel, past or present, at these sites. Please take affirmative steps to ensure that these records are preserved in their current form. Specifically, we ask that you retain any records of hiring, requests for leave, assignment rosters, duty rosters, disciplinary records, records which are used to track EEOC-related or Affirmative Action related data, and any other records related to the allegations as you currently understand them, or past allegations of a similar nature, regardless of who made them or when they were made. The records and things to preserve include notes, forms, personnel data, analog recordings of images, sounds, or other data; digital recordings of images, sounds, or other data; notes, reports, letters, drafts, e-mail, and memoranda; database components, including tables, indices, memos, and queries; electronically created or stored files; electronically created or stored backup files and electronically created or stored backup fragments; all logs related to all such documents.

Thank you for your assistance in ensuring a complete and thorough investigation.

Sincerely,
*Fran A. Sepler, President*
*Sepler & Associates*

# Index